The Future of
Whiteness

For my family

The Future of Whiteness

Linda Martín Alcoff

polity

First published in 2015 by Polity Press

Polity Press
65 Bridge Street
Cambridge CB2 1UR, UK

Polity Press
350 Main Street
Malden, MA 02148, USA

ISBN-13: 978-0-7456-8544-1
ISBN-13: 978-0-7456-8545-8(pb)

A catalogue record for this book is available from the British Library.

Library of Congress Cataloging-in-Publication Data

Alcoff, Linda.
    The future of whiteness / Linda Alcoff.
      pages cm
    ISBN 978-0-7456-8544-1 (hardcover : alk. paper) – ISBN 0-7456-8544-7 (hardcover : alk. paper) – ISBN 978-0-7456-8545-8 (pbk. : alk. paper) – ISBN 0-7456-8545-5 (pbk. : alk. paper) 1. Whites–United States. 2. United States–Race relations. I. Title.
      E184.A1.A46 2015
      305.800973–dc23
                          2015007622

Typeset in 11/13pt on Sabon
by Toppan Best-set Premedia Limited
Printed and bound in the United States by Courier Digital Solutions, North Chelmsford, MA

For further information on Polity, visit our website: politybooks.com

Contents

Acknowledgments

I am very much indebted to all those friends and colleagues who gave me feedback, suggested sources, shared their views with frankness, and offered their encouragement: Bill Bywater, Omar Dahbour, Arlene Dávila, Cate Fosl, Peter Fosl, Kathryn Gines, Leigh Johnson, Chad Kautzer, David Kim, Frank Kirkland, Emily Lee, Donna Dale Marcano, Charles Mills, Michael Monahan, Darrell Moore, Mickaella Perina, Mariana Ortega, Lucius Outlaw, Falguni Sheth, Jaideep Singh, Ron Sundstrum, Paul Taylor, George Yancy, and the impressive activists from SURJ, Showing up for Racial Justice. I also want to note some of my own personal heroes who inspired this work from way back when: Mark Alfonso, Betty Bryant, Pat Bryant, Mary Joyce Carlson, Jehu Eaves, Chele Galloway, Joe Goodman, Charlie Orrock, Nan Orrock, Jim Skillman, David Simpson, Sandy Stimpson, Jan Tucker, Janet Wheat, and Marilyn Williams.

I especially want to acknowledge my family in writing such a book as this, including all parts of my transnational, cross-cultural family, far flung and close knit, left and right, atheist and devout, English only and Spanish dominant, spanning the North, the South, and the global South.

As always, Larry Alcoff, Sam Alcoff, and José Alcoff provided steady encouragement, advice, research, and technical assistance, and showed up to deal with potentially hostile audiences. Most importantly, I want to express my loving gratitude to my parents, Ted and Laura Woodward. I could have emerged into adulthood a very different person if I had not had their love, support, and, most importantly, their moral guidance.

My thanks to Random House for permission to reproduce a quote from *The Second Sex* by Simone de Beauvoir (trans. Constance Borde and Sheila Malovany-Chevallier), published by Vintage. Portions of this book have been drawn from an earlier paper entitled "The Future of Whiteness" published in *Living Alterities: Phenomenology, Embodiment, and Race,* edited by Emily Lee, SUNY Press, 2014.

" ... justice can never be done in the midst of injustice. A colonial administrator has no possibility of acting rightly toward the natives, nor a general toward his soldiers; the only solution is to be neither general nor military chief."
Simone de Beauvoir, *The Second Sex* (trans. Constance Borde and Sheila Malovany-Chevallier), 2011

"In the course of history, there comes a time when humanity is called to shift to a new level of consciousness. To reach a higher moral ground. A time when we have to shed our fear and give hope to each other. That time is now."
Wangari Maathai, Nobel Lecture, 2004

Introduction: The Unbearable Whiteness of Being

This is a book about a topic many would rather avoid. That topic is white identity, its difficult past, complicated present, and uncertain future. Before we can consider its future, or jump to the conclusion that whiteness is withering away, fragmenting beyond recognition, or massively expanding the kinds of persons it includes, we need to understand what whiteness is as a social and historical identity among other such identities, whether this single term can even make sense of a grouping so impossibly varied, and how its utility as a term can survive its constantly changing boundaries. We also have to understand how whiteness is lived, and not just how it is ideologically represented or manipulated. It is especially important to consider how it is lived today by those who are coming to repudiate the ideology of white supremacy. "Being white these days," as Nell Painter (2012, 389) has so aptly remarked, "is not what it used to be." In particular, the historical links between the formation of white identity and racism are becoming more difficult to dodge.

Michael Moore is one of those white folks who clearly figured out the wrongness of racism early on in his life. His first real political act was an intervention at the Elks

Club, no less, when he entered a speech contest on the life of Abraham Lincoln. Moore had discovered in 1970 that segregation still held sway at the Elks golf course in Flint Michigan, where a sign announced "CAUCASIANS ONLY" in helpfully capitalized letters. Confused and incensed by discovering what he had thought was just a southern backwardness right in the midst of his northern hometown, Moore became truly livid when he found the same organization sponsoring a contest for the best speech honoring Lincoln. The Elks seemed to be totally oblivious to the contradiction, but Moore, at 16, was not. "They want a speech? I'll give them a speech," he thought to himself. The resultant effort was an essay that sounds like the Moore we have come to know, not too terribly nuanced, but clear and to the point. He called for segregation, a segregation from the Elks Club.

Moore has been one of our bravest social and cultural critics and a role model as a white antiracist, touring college campuses with Cornel West and calling out racism in every movie he's made. For his efforts, he has received numerous and persistent death threats of the sort the authorities call "credible." In his memoir, appropriately titled *Here Comes Trouble*, Moore sermonizes on the topic of bigotry in the first chapter:

> Only cowards use violence. They are afraid that their ideas will not win out in the public arena. They are weak and worried that the people will see their weakness. They are threatened by women, gays, and minorities – minorities, for chrissakes! You know why they're called "minorities"? Because they don't have the power – YOU do! That's why you're called the "majority"! (2011, 29; emphasis in original)

Moore is beseeching whites to relax and reconsider their fears because, after all, they vastly outnumber minorities.

This form of argumentation will soon have to end. Most demographers are predicting that by 2050, though the US Census Bureau says 2042, white European Americans will slip below majority status in the United States. For the first time in its history, the US will be a majority nonwhite nation. Whites will have to jockey for position in a multipolar nation, just as, since the end of the Cold War, they have had to negotiate a decentered, multipolar world. White people all over the world are coming to experience in both their national and global communities what some inelegantly call minoritized status. This demographic phenomenon is by no means restricted to the US: lower birth rates in Europe constitute what has been described as a voluntary demographic suicide. There too, immigrant fertility outflanks that of white Christian Europeans, leading to the prediction that Europe itself will become a majority Muslim continent in the next century. Given these trends, it is understandable if whites are apprehensive about the future.

Reports from the 2010 Census chart the national changes in the United States quite clearly. Between 2000 and 2010, the US population increased by nearly 10 percent to 308 million souls. Latino and Asian numbers jumped the most, with each group growing by a remarkable 43 percent. But African American numbers also climbed 12 percent, and even the category "American Indian and Alaska Native" jumped 18 percent. In contrast, the white population lagged markedly behind, increasing only by 1 percent. Hence, whites lost five points of their market share in the overall population, dropping from 69 percent to 64 percent in just one decade. But even this number is misleading, since the category of "white" used by the 2010 Census included both North Africans and peoples of the Middle East, hardly groups associated with the heartland of America.

The demographers making these predictions are taking all the variables into account, including the fluctuations of the birth rate. The white population is older, other groups tend to be younger, and most of the increase in the numbers of nonwhites are children born in the United States. Nonwhite babies already outnumber white babies. So even if the birth rate were to change dramatically, and immigration was magically stopped, the deed is done.

I argue in this book that this impending change constitutes a specter haunting the United States as well as Europe, producing a white reaction that can take pretty hysterical forms, although it is often carefully cloaked to avoid the charge of racism. The demographic shift is obviously central to strategies of the right, such as the open fascists of Hungary and Greece, but also of centrists and moderates everywhere. It is not an overstatement to say that every major political issue debated in the public domain is affected by this specter, well beyond the immigration debates. In the United States, the changing demographics affects electoral politics at nearly every level, including general reactions to President Obama, as well as debates over tax policy, healthcare, and the purported problem of "voter fraud." Local and global demographic issues entwine over the concern about becoming a debtor nation to China, a nonwhite country. Since whites will retain economic advantages even after they lose majority status, becoming a minority with a majority of the country's wealth, increased inheritance taxes, and redistributive proposals can incite racial animus (Glaser and Ryan 2013). This combination of racial and economic differences is central to the debate over limiting the sale of guns. During Obama's presidency, sales spiked so much that some firearms manufacturers have wittily named him "Gun Salesman of the Year." But the truth is that Obama was a symbol for a larger issue: an impending white minority with a greater share of resources facing off groups whose long history of unfair treatment produced at least some of that collective wealth.

Beyond the economic issues involved in losing majority status, there is an important political one. Holding a significant majority within a nation had granted whites the ability to believe in the legitimacy of a white-dominated government. This apparent justification of white domination will soon disappear. For a long time the collective imaginary of race in the United States involved a black/white binary: the image of a securely massive white population facing off against mainly a black population, with negligible numbers of other *others*. African Americans, the largest minority until 2003, were never imagined to balloon in numbers sufficient to unseat the white majority. This black/white imaginary has stymied race analysis and the maturation of antiracist politics: it is one thing to feel benevolent toward a minority who will always be a minority, but quite another to negotiate on equal terms with powerful groups who together hold the majority.

While the impending demographic changes have unleashed a *Sturm und Drang* among the white right (including neo-conservatives, Tea Partyers, neo-Nazis, and everything in between), the white-dominated left, from liberal to progressive, including even the moderate wing of the Republican Party, has been mostly reticent to speculate publicly on what this future will mean for the United States. As Desmond S. King and Rogers M. Smith (2011) have noted, "on race, the silence is bipartisan." Everything from the economic crisis to the political divide demands an analysis of race, as they point out, yet white liberals remain uncomfortable in broaching the topic, while conservatives generally try to disguise their racial references, though the disguise is often so ineffective as to be a joke.

Opportunities abound for a serious discussion of how the changing demographics may change this country, but are too often deftly sidestepped. Major left-wing public intellectuals, including Francis Fox Piven, analyzed Occupy Wall Street movements as transcending the era of identity politics to place class front and square, as if class could be understood separately from race. So the result is that the extreme unabashed right wing dominates race-talk, while all others, including the left, the liberals, and the moderates, largely maintain race avoidance.

This may be motivated by the idea, or the worry, that if we talk about demographic changes directly, we invite reprisal, feeding the flames of white reaction. We should not, some reason, portray these impending changes as important to discuss. Some whites may fear that a focus on demographic changes will appear to be intrinsically racist, since this would be to acknowledge the importance of a category – race – that we should, they think, be trying to overcome. Such avoidance strategies may also be motivated by white liberals who have become too accustomed to placating the racist in the family gathering, thinking that if they avoid the subject, he (or she) won't have an excuse to spout idiocies. And there is also a recurring concern that race-talk can be overplayed, that the mainstream's late acknowledgment of "dog-whistle politics," or the fact that our public discourses are peppered with covert appeals to race, has lately become an overused explanation, a distortion of legitimate debates about fiscal policy, or a defensive maneuver of Obama defenders (Chait 2014).

Yet clearly, we cannot even engage in the debate about when race applies and when it doesn't while there is so much energy spent preempting the discussion. Unless we talk about these demographic changes up front, we cannot plausibly claim to know how they affect social trends and political debates.

Much of the mainstream left, which has long been white-dominated (simply because of demographics, but also because of its tendency to separate class from race), has made a frontal assault on identity politics for decades, making life uncomfortable for anyone daring to defend the relevance of identity to politics. This assault, together with the academy's skeptical disclaimers about the concept of race, has left many unable to analyze or even address the imminent demographic changes in the racial make-up of the country and how this is impacting our public culture. If race is basically an illusion – or a mere ideological overlay that mystifies reality, as it is on this mainstream left view – then the demographic changes make no real difference, only a difference at the level of ideology. Marx sarcastically accused Hegel of portraying social antagonisms as mere battles of ideas fighting it out in the air. If one thinks "race" is nothing but an illusion, one might well apply this charge to the fights over race.

For decades now, some of the most radical white theorists have been arguing for the abolition of whiteness, given the illusory nature of racial categories (see Livingstone 1962; Warnke 2007). If race is illusory, then the coming changes in population distributions should be treated as meaningless. If, as influential historian David Roediger puts it (1994), race concepts of all sorts are "ontologically empty," then the task is not to take the coming changes seriously but to show why they make no difference.

The racial identity we call whiteness has been especially disavowed by some quarters of the white left on the grounds that it is a political construct that does nothing more than cloak the plutocracy. We should be tearing away the cloak, they argue, not giving into the idea that whiteness is real.

Yet this sort of approach simply bolsters the avoidance of race-talk or of engaging with the critical question of the demographic shifts. Further, as I will argue in this book, this repudiation of race-talk may in actuality be an indication of a basic discomfort with being white. Whiteness is not cool, it is not on the right side of history, and it is associated with many troubling dispositions, most importantly racism. If one doesn't want to take the chauvinist route of defending whiteness against these charges, then why would anyone in their right mind want to be associated with whiteness?

But we need to find out whether the actual politics of white identity and of white people fits the stereotype. Is it really the case that the main response of white people to a loss of majority status will be racism, fear, anger, and violence – in short, reaction? That economically struggling whites will forever identify more with the 1 percent than with the multiracial majority? Such fatalistic responses may seem to gain credence from new social histories tracing the lineage of the very concept of white identity to racism and white supremacy, portraying whiteness itself as a plot to demobilize class consciousness. If white identity cannot be separated from this foundation in white racial dominance – if to avow one's whiteness is to buy into the ideology – then whites who convert to an antiracist social view have no other option than to disavow their white identity.

Whiteness As Real, and Really Open-Ended

This makes no sense to me. Even in the far distant future, when we might imagine white supremacy as a material and ideological practice to have come to a long-deserved end, whites may well still exist, at least for a while. Whiteness is, after all, produced by a complex of historical events, rather than a single originary moment (see e.g. Cash 1941; Frye 1992; Delgado and Stefancic 1997; Domínguez 1997). And history has a long reach. Thus, whiteness is far from ontologically empty: it is a historically emergent lived experience, variegated, changing, and changeable. Being white is a powerfully important element in one's life, just as is not being white. But in the view I will develop in this book, whiteness as a term is not coterminous with dominance, but with a particular historical experience and relationship to certain historical events. Among other things, every white person in the Americas or Australia has some relationship to a family history of immigration, and the large majority of this immigration was economically motivated. This formative aspect of whiteness is hardly unique, and thus should raise questions about the boundaries as well as the content of whiteness, given the similarity whites have with most other immigrants (Jacobson 1998). Against Bonilla-Silva's (2006) influential claim about the expanded borders of whiteness today, however, I want to insist that whiteness has a very particular and unique relationship to historical atrocities such as slavery and the genocide of native peoples. Even though whites differ widely in their affective orientation to these events, there is a distinction between their likely assorted affective responses (such as shame, guilt, denial) and those whose families were indigenous and subject to genocide or to slavery or to imperial wars in which the US played a leading part. This produces a content to whiteness despite its immense variety and moveable boundaries.

But it is one thing to say that we need a radical re-understanding of what whiteness means, and what whites have in common with many nonwhites (such as immigration histories), and another altogether to say that whiteness has no meaning at all. If our image of an antiracist future is a future in which white identity no longer exists, this means that whites will no longer know who they are. And the claim that they have abolished their whiteness may well provide an alibi for the mistaken belief that the unearned social and economic advantages accrued by white skin are a thing of the past.

A more reasonable approach is to understand whiteness as an organically emergent phenomenon. Its economic and political power can be measured by social scientists, its arrival as a commonly used term can be dated by historians, and its characteristic subjective contours can be discerned through the experiments of social psychology. There is a facticity of whiteness, whether or not it factors into a person's self-ascription. Whiteness is lived, and not merely represented. It is a prominent feature of one's way of being in the world, of how one navigates that world, and of how one is navigated around by others.

Whiteness should not be reduced to racism or even racial privilege, even though these have been central aspects of what it means to be white. No social identity can be defined by a single vector across every possible context, and even white identity constitutes a social disadvantage in some situations. Moreover, today, perhaps more than ever, whiteness has a variegated relationship to avowed racism. About half of whites agree with most people of color on many issues related to race, including the claim that antiblack racism is still a large problem, that racism infects the criminal justice system, and that immigrants are treated unfairly. For example, according to Pew Research Center data from 2014, only 48 percent of whites believe that "a lot" of progress has been made on racism; that leaves 52 percent who believe that either little or no progress has been made. Only 35 percent of whites have "a great deal" of confidence in the police. Now this leaves a more than 20-point gap between how black Americans respond to this question, but the interesting point is that 65 percent of whites disagreed with this claim and, in fact, only 36 percent of whites say they have a great deal of confidence that police officers in their community will not use excessive force and will treat blacks and whites equally. We focus too often on the gap between white and black and brown, and miss the growing gap among whites. The nation is increasingly politically polarized on a number of critical issues, from guns to healthcare, and that polarization is mainly due to the polarization occurring among whites themselves.

The question is how to understand this phenomenon. Historical and sociological work in whiteness studies has built up a strong case for the constitutive relation between whiteness and racism. Besides Roediger, there is the work of W. E. B. Du Bois (1986), Langston Hughes (1933), George Lipsitz (1998), Joe Feagin and colleagues (2001); Feagin (2013), Bruce Baum (2006), Jessie Daniels (1997), and others who have persuasively traced the historical formation of white identity to the political ploys by elites to divide and conquer the working masses. More recently, social psychologists and sociologists such as Claude Steele (2010), Charles Gallagher (1994), Michael Tesler and David Sears (2010), and Jennifer Richeson and Sophie Trawalter (2008), as well as philosophers Shannon Sullivan (2005), Charles Mills (1997), and George Yancy (2008), among others, have begun to measure the legacy this long history has wrought in the unconscious habits as well as conscious attitudes and political beliefs of the people who came to see themselves as white. Persistent and unfair economic advantages generated an epistemology of ignorance, as Charles Mills has named it, among those who had little interest in questioning the irrational foundations of race-talk. Shannon Sullivan has explored the distinctive bodily comportment practices that whites exhibit, such as their assumptions about being entitled to all public spaces and to inhabit, and move into, any and every neighborhood. White political attitudes have been disposed toward a communitarianism based on race rather than a solidarity based on class. This translates into an assumption by poor whites that they are entitled to a share of the fat of the land in a way others are not.

In truth, the formation of white identity was not merely a ploy, but an identity category that helpfully filled a void created by the European diaspora and cross-ethnic amalgamations. The ability to sustain strong and substantive ethnic identifications and self-ascriptions – "German," "Norwegian," "Scottish" – across multiple generations of immigrants living in the new world was surely doomed by long geographical distance and interethnic mixing. Moreover, many European immigrants did not leave their home countries by choice: rather, they were summarily booted out by starvation wages, if not political, ethnic, or religious violence. To be tagged by identity terms like "Polish American" or "Lithuanian American" reminded such groups of histories many wanted to forget, especially if other Poles and Lithuanians had forced their families to leave. These groups wanted to transcend their old identities by coming to a place where they might achieve not only an economic livelihood, but an improved social status, perhaps even a social equality. The idea of whiteness ingeniously filled an identity gap produced by the distaste for and diffusion of ethnic and national European attachments, and filled it in a way that served the interests of elites; just think how different it might have been if this working mob had been interpellated simply by a national identity that would have united people across continents of origin, if they had maintained the bonds of workplace solidarity that Peter Linebaugh and Marcus Rediker (2000) show to have existed, at times, in the eighteenth century. Chattel slavery, and the development of inherited enslavement based on color, broke those bonds. Race, an idea already powerful in the West, moved to the fore, giving a name to the differential experiences people had upon their arrival in the Americas, while also, without a doubt, allowing the plutocrats to divide the servant class.

Still, the transformation into a self-ascribed whiteness was neither smooth nor uniform. Whiteness was an idea that was promoted, yes, but it had to be shaped by those who ascribed to it to fit their own experience and understanding. Whiteness has always had varied meanings and effects depending on time and place, from the Irish mill-workers of the South to the Scandinavian farmers of the Midwest to the polyglot meatpackers of Chicago and the southern Europeans who flooded into Levittown. Whiteness was in every case a different ethnic mix, with sometimes quite different associated ways of life, from fighting and drinking to abstinence and asceticism to consumerism and conformity. But in all cases, being white was part of what these people became, part of how their characteristics were interpreted and judged, part of how their economic options were organized. Blackness was neither the only nor the most important contrast in every case. Sometimes the more relevant other was Indian, Mexican, or Chinese, and this too changed the particularities that whiteness came to manifest.

The ferment we are experiencing in white identity today is simply the most recent, but hardly the first. When southern Europeans, the Irish, and Jews "became" white in the early years of the twentieth century, there was similar ferment about what this meant for the peer-based ethics of racially segregated communities, in which intragroup ethics varied, sometimes quite drastically, from intergroup ethics, or how people were allowed, and even expected, to treat those outside their own racial group. As Russell Banks recounts, consolidated acceptance of this enlarged white identity was far from complete when he was growing up in the 1940s and 50s:

> My father and other Anglo-American men of his generation used to refer to Italians as "Guineas." I never knew what a Guinea was until I was an adult and saw that it was a nineteenth-century word for Africa, and thus for Africans. What that means is that as recently as the 1950s Italians and other Mediterraneans were seen as racially different from us white folks. (2008, 32)

Arguably, southern Europeans and Jews are even today only borderline whites, culturally marked as distinct and problematic, with less evidence of the mythical values of honesty, cool-headedness, and hard work associated with Protestants. The number of white supremacists who use the swastika as their favorite symbol indicates that not everyone with light skin tones gets to count. Today, we are all watching the huge influx of eastern Europeans to see whether they will be assimilated, whether they will want to assimilate, and how they will change what it means to be white.

Nonetheless, the ideology of whiteness urged Americans from the beginning of the twentieth century to understand race as more significant than ethnic differences, and to extend peer-based respect, including courtesy and at least formal equality, to Italians, Jews, Greeks, Poles, the Irish, and other heretofore derided European ethnic groups. This initiated decades of cultural contestations over inclusion policies and political constituencies, manifested not only in neighborhood relations such as those described by Banks, but also in the working coalitions of electoral politics, union locals, and hiring halls. Officially, the job listings changed from "No Irish Need Apply" to "White Men Wanted," and fraternity and country club rules loosened around a multiplicity of ethnic whites. Nonwhites, and all women, could be excluded from job listings up through the 1960s, but the infamous ethnic-based exclusions common in the earlier part of the century were slowly diminished, at least in their overt forms.

To include such derided groups within one's own identity ascription meant changing the self-perceptions of British and other northern European whites and their long-held sense of cultural superiority over southern Europeans. Even today in Europe, it is common to hear the countries of Portugal, Italy, Greece, and Spain collectively referred to by the insulting acronym "PIGS." In the United States as well, the Irish and southern Europeans are still marked as different by the phrase "white ethnics," a term never used for whites with an English, French, or German lineage. Racial interpellation may have subordinated ethnic chauvinism, but in no way was it erased.

Such contestations over white ethnic out-groups were still going on when the African American civil rights movement erupted in mid-century in towns across the country and on national television, creating a second major period of ferment over what it meant to be white. The new national television media revealed with visual intensity that the country's nonwhite others were mobilizing for a full and meaningful franchise, with demands backed by strong moral and religious arguments and a collective of youth willing to die for the cause. Some whites were genuinely convinced by these arguments and supported civil rights, though many were fearful about the emerging political power of the grandchildren of slaves. If any group had a moral claim on the nation, surely this group had one that could not be rationally denied. As Howard Winant has noted, civil rights "deeply affected whites as well as blacks, exposing and denouncing often unconscious beliefs in white supremacy, and demanding new and more respectful forms of behavior in relation to nonwhites" (1997, 41). Suze Rotolo, Bob Dylan's girlfriend in the 1960s, put it more bluntly: "Pure unadulterated white racism," she recounts, was "splattered all over the media as the violence against the civil rights workers escalated. White people were looking at themselves and what their history had wrought, like a domestic animal having its face shoved into its own urine" (2008, 87).

To retain its moral self-respect in the face of this moral movement, whiteness had to redeem itself by becoming liberal and inclusive. Predictably, this generally took a paternalistic form, retaining as much white supremacy as possible, while giving way, a bit. The southern white racists visible on television screens across the country throwing rocks at schoolchildren and bricks at ministers could not plausibly embody white moral and intellectual superiority, even for most white people. Many whites found themselves experiencing a disidentification with the Klan types who were claiming to represent and defend the rights and interests of white people, and some began to develop a dawning empathy for the Klan's targets. Marginal whites who had experienced their own share of ethnic chauvinism were no doubt especially ready to see the lies of white supremacy. For these disidentified whites, whiteness had to become something other than the violent maintenance of antiblack social codes.

Thus whiteness is, as I will outline in Chapter 1, a historical and social construct that has persistently undergone change. It is not a singular idea, but a fluid amalgam of sometimes contesting interpretations and practices. White supremacy is itself incoherent, and can manifest itself quite differently depending on historical periods and social groups: from Klan violence to law-backed disenfranchisement to paternal scolding that blames victims for their "culture of poverty" to entitled gentrifications of neighborhoods that force the nonwhite poor out of cities with an indifferent shrug.

Bruce Norris's Pulitzer Prize-winning play *Clybourne Park* (2011) exposes the racism of contemporary whites who assume they are entitled to the most desirable neighborhoods, and deftly, with the help of fellow playwright Lorraine Hansberry, skewers the older era's cross-burning racists. His play's cross-generational snapshots of whites ranging from the 1950s to the present reveal differences of tone and discourse, but also a similarity of effect: some are unwilling to live among black people no matter what the economic cost is to themselves, while others find integrated living perfectly agreeable as long as their presumptions of superiority are never called out. The moral of Norris's story is not, however, that whiteness and racism have remained exactly the same across the 50-year span the play covers. In 1959 African Americans were largely invisible servants, while in 2010 they are portrayed as neighbors whose reasoning is simply unintelligible to white gentrifiers. Whites then had no need for dialogue with or acceptance from African Americans: today this has changed. The fact that this story is told so well by a white playwright should suggest the dramatic political divergence among whites. The truth is that these divergences of knowledge as well as of values and political commitments have always existed within white communities, and exploring their implications is an important task of any analysis of whiteness. Norris is no less white for his perceptive analysis of racism; in fact, it is his very whiteness that most likely renders his portraits so recognizable.

Whiteness from Below

The historical narrative of whiteness as a form of false consciousness foisted from above with uniform results has been challenged by newer studies that highlight these internal divisions, mostly based on class, but also on ethnic, divisions. For example, Linebaugh and Rediker's (2000) award-winning study of early American cross-race class alliances helped seriously to upend the bleak characterization of white working-class identifications. The "many-headed hydra" of their book title was a term used in the 1700s to refer to rebelliousness that took multiple forms, from food-rioters, to heretics, to army-agitators, to pirates, to "rural barbarians of the commons" and "motley urban mobs" (2000, 329). This represents a lost history of class-based resistance, but, just as importantly, Linebaugh and Rediker also unearthed a complexity of identity configurations belied by our uniform categories. In other words, all "whites" did not either think or act alike, or have similar experiences. The fact that this history has been largely lost is no coincidence, they suggest, but an element of the orchestration of whiteness itself as an identity that is meant to organize society, explain history, and trump class. In an analysis compatible with Ernesto Laclau and Chantal Mouffe's (1985) emphasis on the historical variability of political identity, Linebaugh and Rediker show that race-based groups and hierarchies trumped class less than we often suppose. Michael Monahan's account (2011) of racialization processes in the English Caribbean is similarly focused on the period when Irish indentured servants were bonded in service in conditions comparable to their African contemporaries. At least some such bonded servants managed to join together across their diverse identities of origin in mutual acts of support.

Though Monahan shies away from calling the bonded Irish laborers of the new world "slaves," Nell Painter (2010) uses precisely this term to emphasize the common conditions of bonded labor before the development of race-based slavery took effect, driving a secure wedge between poor communities. Interestingly, whereas Linebaugh and Rediker, in their effort to complicate our picture of early American labor, want to downplay the whiteness, or white identities, of the early modern European immigrant workers they discuss, both Painter and Monahan make clear that the category of whiteness was operating even in these early days well before the American Revolution, even before the term itself was regularly used. They also show that, despite some significant commonalities across different racial groups, there were also significant differences in the experience of immigration for whites and nonwhites, and these differences were eventually used to sharply distinguish their options for escaping bondage. For example, English Members of Parliament were concerned that enslaving the Irish might produce a domino effect of brutality, a concern they did not voice about "Negroes." For Painter and Monahan, whiteness was not determined by self-ascription. Rather, its existence can be discerned by sociological analysis: European bonded labor had a different trajectory because it was positioned differently vis-à-vis the propertied class.

In sum, these new histories trouble the idea both that whiteness was a moniker only emerging in the late nineteenth century with no critical purchase on social life before it was officially recognized by the state, and also that whiteness served to mandate a primary set of allegiances for all who came under its banner. Whiteness affected one's life options even before it became an official category, but it did not always determine allegiances. This is just to say that whiteness then was not too different from what whiteness is now.

Another book that complicates common generalizations about white workers comes from Amy Sonnie and James Tracy (2011), two contemporary activists determined to tell the untold story of white identified rebels in the 1960s. They recount a little-known history of white activists who found themselves in the midst of urban rebellions against white supremacy. These were not the middle-class white allies who supported civil rights, but poor whites who created their own self-described organizations in both the North and the South to join in a coalitional effort to "fight the power" on behalf of their own communities. Groups such as the Young Patriots, Rising Up Angry, the October 4th Organization, and White Lightening developed antiracist agendas that brought them into allegiance with the Panthers, the Young Lords, the Student Nonviolent Coordinating Committee (SNCC), the Congress of Racial Equality (CORE), and other black- and brown-led organizations. Sonnie and Tracy emphasize how much this history has been neglected:

> Until recently, the narrative of the Sixties New Left largely excluded serious mention of poor and working class whites who formed or took over radical organizations. Instead, historians have tended to focus on the oppositional role of white workers – Teamsters, construction workers, carpenters – who violently confronted anti-war protesters, disregarded the plight of fellow Black and Brown workers, and cajoled labor's support for US military actions in Vietnam and Cambodia. (2011, 5)

The reactionary sector of the white workforce, sympathetically portrayed in the television hit *All in the Family*, with its "likable" bigot Archie Bunker, was in truth being contested by another sector of white workers who were organizing with explicitly antiracist, pro-working-class politics. Importantly, they were organized as identity-based groups – run by poor whites for poor whites – just as the nonwhite groups had come to be at this stage of the movement. But they maintained a determined allegiance with radical organizations of color, just as many of the latter groups, even many firmly nationalist ones, also held cross-race coalition to be a principled strategy despite favoring segregated political organizations. Most significantly, the white groups described by Sonnie and Tracy joined the radical movements of the 1960s as actors struggling for their own interests, and not merely as allies supporting social causes on behalf of others. They developed symbols and forms of discourse that drew on a specifically white semiotic toward revolutionary ends, with ducktail pomaded hairstyles, white shirts with rolled-up sleeves, even using the Confederate flag to signal a white aesthetic.

Based on this complicated history of whiteness, this book will argue against the inevitability of white reaction and against the idea that white identity cannot adapt in positive ways to a loss of centrality. It is not at all clear that, without white supremacy, there can be no whiteness.

Just as the history of whiteness evinces variation, so too, no doubt, will its future. But we need an account of what whiteness can possibly mean apart from white supremacy, given its strong and long-lasting connection to supremacist ideologies, if we want to make that future more imaginatively real. Otherwise, if we imagine that whiteness is truly and irrevocably constituted by racism, then the claim that whiteness will persist into the future is a claim of defeat. I will argue that this essentializing of whiteness as necessarily, fundamentally, and centrally about white supremacy is simply ahistorical, and based on a wrong understanding of how meanings operate as well as of how social identities are formed.

The problematic category of race that seems to be necessarily implied by the category of whiteness is no doubt another principal block against imagining a future use of the term. Racial terms of all sorts have been defined as biological categories in a way that scientists now agree is highly misleading, to put it mildly. As Ashley Montagu put it decades ago, "race" is the "phlogiston of our time" (quoted in Baum 2006, 214). Why not, then, move to ethnic terms, or national terms, or anything else other than the outdated and biologically misleading concept of race?

"Race"

Despite the fact that the concept of race is biologically baseless, I will have an extended argument in Chapter 3 against either the possibility or the advisability of trying to dispense with the category of white identity at this historical point. Race has a historical association with biological claims, but biological essences are not always what is meant by race-terms. Just consider the variable ways in which W. E. B. Du Bois used the term over his lifetime. In common parlance today, race concepts are often used to refer to groupings that are visibly demarcated and socially significant, with a shared geographical lineage. People on the street are not always thinking DNA when they talk about the make-up of a night club or a sports team or a neighborhood.

This everyday way of using race-terms can merge into ethnic differentiations, and the efforts of governments, social scientists, and political philosophers to keep these categories neatly distinguishable is no doubt useless. As Victoria Hattam notes (2007, 10), the effort definitively and systematically to establish a separation between ethnicity and race exhibits an "anxious obsessive quality" more revealing about our anxieties over difference than our acceptance of the inevitable fluid uncertainties in which group differences are articulated, not to mention lived. In rejecting group concepts, what many people want, I'd suggest, is control: to have agency over their identity, rendering it subject to volitional commitments more in the manner of nationality (ostensibly). Being identified in a way that lies beyond our individual control conflicts with individualist ideas, and illusions, about our autonomy. The real concern with race may be less the faulty presumptions about genetic difference than the fact that this is a social fact about us, with social meanings and implications over which we have limited agency. People of color have largely come to accept this; for whites, the forcible interpellations of their racial identity are more often a new experience.

Hence, whiteness, as I will argue, does not need to be a meaningful biological category for it to designate a meaningful social and historical category with sometimes unwanted and irrational material effects. Yet, like all other racialized identities, whiteness is also constantly in the process of dynamic reinterpretation and internal contestation, and the future of its material effects is, particularly today, in some doubt.

Concepts constantly change in meaning, and the loss of a biological definition does not necessarily mean that the concept of race will not survive. If we think about whiteness as a historically embedded or contextual sociological category, we can read the social history of whiteness not as the history of false consciousness or delusions about biology but as the history of a group formation. Like other group formations, whiteness has often been mythically rendered, its actual history truncated to foreground the good bits. This doesn't mean that whiteness doesn't exist. The workers who developed cross-racial unity as described in Sonnie and Tracy's study did not thereby lose or diminish their whiteness, even while they were contesting what whiteness means in relation to privilege or domination. They took both their class and their race to be relevant to political mobilization, as it undoubtedly was in that historical context. By creating political organizations as and for poor whites, they could mark their specific position in US society, contest the false claims of class mobility within the white category, and participate in the struggle for social change with nonwhite groups in a way that made sense.

The truth is that whiteness is not an illusion but a historically evolving identity-formation that is produced in diverse locations, while constantly undergoing reinterpretation and contestation. Its evolution does not follow a pattern of uplift, rationality, consistency, or increasing inclusiveness. Legally, for example, whiteness has at times, and in some states, included Latinos, while in others it has not, and the trajectory of these historical shifts has not taken a developmentally progressive form but a back-and-forth movement that can look pretty chaotic (Haney-López 2006; Martinez 1997; Hattam 2007). In Texas, Latinos were classified as white at one point so that courts could get round having to appoint Latinos to juries with Latino defendants: as long as Latinos were classified as white, then an all-Anglo jury – i.e. even with no Latino members – could be described as "a jury of their peers," which no defense attorney could contest. Despite the ambiguous relationship Latinos have had to the category of whiteness, Latinos are arguably worse off today in Arizona and other parts of the Southwest than they were in the past, where the national trends of wage theft, accidents on the job in unsafe conditions, and violence against the undocumented are all on the rise (Telles and Ortiz 2008). Today, officially, according to the US Census, Arabs and persons from the Middle East are classified as white and are hence barred from affirmative action or other minority set-asides, despite the intense levels of prejudice and discrimination they have experienced since 9/11. Hence, when minorities are included officially as "white," this does not necessarily make their political and economic condition better than or comparable to white averages. There are no grounds to predict with certainty how the borders of whiteness will shift, or whether those who are temporarily included will be better off.

Even with this internal diversity and these mobile borders, however, whiteness has real, measurable, material, and psychological effects. Whiteness operates as a kind of property, as Cheryl Hall (1995) has put it, with effects on social confidence and performance that can be empirically documented. Whiteness has not always had the same meaning, or included the same people, or sustained unquestioned allegiance among its designated members, but it has been a reality in both the subjective and objective aspects of social existence.

The Future is an Ought as well as an Is

Precisely because of its contingency and historically dynamic character, we cannot assume that we can know a priori all the future permutations that whiteness may take. It is certainly useless to engage in utopian dreaming while ignoring empirical realities, but it is downright harmful to assume that the future is closed, either because we think we know things will get progressively better by some Whiggish/Hegelian law of necessity, even in the absence of effective social movements, or because we think we know the absolute, logical constraints on the flexibility of racial concepts. I want to underscore the fact that whiteness is not simply a concept, but a complex identity-formation;

this is important since it means we cannot simply analyze the concept, but must consider the actual lived social identity in a full sense in all its varied permutations. We can assume neither that whiteness will forever remain tethered to racism nor that whiteness will peaceably adapt to its changed status once it loses the majority. Ironically, such epistemic hubris in either direction – toward optimism or pessimism – is endemic to the problematic aspects that white identity has historically manifested, in assuming a capacity to know and control the future.

To take the future of white identity to be open is to leave unanswered the question of how whites will face living in the very different kind of society that will ensue. The question of how they should adapt to the new loss of majority status seems much more obvious: whites should adapt to a multiracial, decentralized society in the same basic way that others have, by not assuming a right of presumptive entitlement to political leadership, cultural domination, or comparative economic prosperity – by learning, in short, to share, to take a turn on the periphery now and again, and, most importantly, to learn more about the others with whom they cohabit nations. Yet the obstacles to achieving such modest goals are, admittedly, legion, given how different white identity is from other forms of ethnic and racial identities that have come to the United States never expecting to rule it. White identity has not had to share much of anything. It has been inculcated with a vanguardist illusion for over a century that has configured European whites as the scientific, technological, moral, artistic, and political leader of the human race.

We continue to hear the reverberations of this project every time a president – any president – announces the exceptional American capacity (and right) to lead the world in the expansion of democracy, freedom, and prosperity. The psychic benefit to white-designated people of this characterization as the global vanguard continues to pay dividends even when the actual economic benefits are increasingly negligible for the majority of whites, as Du

Bois argued as early as 1935 in *Black Reconstruction in America*. Thus, although all racialized identities are social and historical constructs, the construction of whiteness has taken a specific form that poses unique and daunting challenges for an adaptation to minority citizenship and to living alongside others in relations of equality.

Nonetheless, change is inevitable. The impending demographic events will undoubtedly transform how whiteness is understood, how we interpret its history, and how it can be lived. Whiteness will no longer be invisible when the majority of Americans find it so very visible in its foregrounded status as the newest minority. It will no longer be a default identity for leadership, nor will it be able to justify its cultural hegemony. Those who want to maintain the traditional vanguard meanings of whiteness will have to operate in a netherworld of imagined dominance, since real dominance will become a mere memory. They may nonetheless decide to circle their wagons in increasingly small and isolated communities, nostalgically preferring the dreamworld of the past, while refusing to engage the realities of the present. Yet even Civil War re-enactors and "Medieval Faire" enthusiasts are finding their hobby spaces integrated.

Already, more integrated public spheres in which whites work and go to school are slowly though noticeably altering the spectrum of family formation. Both the Bush and the Obama families have mixed race families, after all. The growing percentage of white families that cross race lines has produced a new impetus for changed self-perceptions. The paternal attitudes of white liberals in the 1960s was predicated on maintaining a distinction: they hoped the racial Other experienced social uplift and integration, but that there would still be clear social, cultural, and psychological boundaries and, hence, whiteness would not change fundamentally. This is what is beginning to erode. White families are not always so white anymore. Nor do whites themselves clearly exude an exclusivist pattern of normative behavioral whiteness. This is true not just in relation to their cultural tastes and preferences, but also in their way of being in the world. Even the so-called "dysfunctional" cultures attributed to black and brown families are now being attributed to the white poor. The ever controversial Charles Murray (2012) argues that the culture of poverty has crossed the color line. His analysis of white poverty is astoundingly uninformed, and victim-blaming, but his account exhibits these boundary breakdowns in the way the poor of all races are viewed and treated. Such treatment is no doubt altering many white sensibilities and affective ties.

The ferment we are witnessing today thus has some new elements. However, we must resist the temptation to relax into a confident assurance that the future will be better than the past, or that we will evolve smoothly toward resolving all present-day conflicts in an integrated utopia that transcends racialization. In truth, things can get worse instead of better, as the lessons of many white minority nations from southern Africa to Latin America demonstrate. In truth, we cannot know with any certainty what the future will bring, other than that there will be a change in the numbers. Surely our current identity categories will be transformed, but racism and chauvinism can mutate into forms that fly under the radar and resist the best arguments we currently have.

Although I argue that we must recognize this open character of the future, I also argue in this book that neither the total elimination nor the effective deconstruction of race is visible on the next horizon. The persistence of whiteness as an aspect of identity is not an open question. It is not withering away or fragmenting beyond all recognition. Centuries of preferences for white skin are not so easily turned to dust, and, in fact, the aesthetic preference for lighter skin is still in a stage of global expansion, as lightening creams (with sometimes toxic ingredients) find new markets in Thailand and Brazil. White supremacy is built into our material culture, from our neighborhood schools, to our university faculty, to our business and scientific leadership, to our historic sites and statues, to the contents that fill our most well-funded museums and libraries, to the portraits that dominate our public buildings. White reaction to nonwhite political emergence is more organized, more armed, and more insidious in its discursive double-speak about race-blind justice and the intransigence of "cultural" difference (Haney-López 2014).

Most importantly, because real estate remains the largest source of wealth for most Americans, and because of our liberal inheritance laws, white economic privilege vis-à-vis other groups who became middle class much more recently will continue for generations beyond these current and impending demographic shifts. The 2008 economic crisis in real estate hit homeowners of color particularly hard, costing them between $146 billion and $190 billion, according to estimates from United for a Fair Economy, and throwing millions back into rental property. The specter of South Africa, where concentrations of white wealth have survived the loss of white political hegemony, stands as a real possibility for the future of the United States.

The specter of South America, where colorism maintains light-skinned dominance even while there is ubiquitous racial mixing, is another possible future. There are no grounds to assume that an easy, inevitable, progression of racial equality will slowly accede to the forefront. It is true that corporations increasingly understand the desirability of drawing from multiple groups when searching for managerial leaders and research and design experts, but this does not translate into meaningful changes in the wage structure at the heavy multiracial bottom of the pyramid, for the bus drivers, nurse aids, deliverymen, gardeners, hotel maids, childcare workers, nannies, domestics, construction workers, dishwashers, short order cooks, doormen, store clerks, cafeteria workers, luggage handlers, prison guards, traffic cops, road crews, poultry workers, farm workers, or the rest of the workforce at the "back of the house" who serve this society. More people of color at the top does not translate into positive progress for the masses of nonwhite workers, and here I would strongly disagree with more optimistic demographers such as Richard Alba (2009). Businesses can diversify the professional managerial class and still use the cloak of "market realities" to underpay most nonwhite workers. And as a result, the pay of white workers who work alongside them will remain similarly deflated. In fact, the diversification of management can be motivated precisely by the need to more effectively manage, and maintain dominance over, the nonwhite workforce. There is no inevitability to a cheerful future in which race loses its economic effects on one's likely livelihood, or on that livelihood's typical pay scale. In fact, there are concrete obstacles warning of quite the reverse.

Thus, the significant material infrastructure of whiteness – which we should understand as including its psychic as well as its material wages – indicates that whiteness is not about to disappear. This book will take a close look at the proclamation that we are on our way to a post-racial, cosmopolitan, de-racialized future, and show why this is a pipe dream. Social identities – including racial ones – are sedimentations of history and formative of subjectivity. They are also, as Satya Mohanty (1997) has argued, explanatory forces for understanding and navigating one's social world. The category of whiteness will continue for some time to be formative of subjectivity, and remains a necessary category to explain our history as well as to navigate our immediate environments. Despite the moving borders and altered meanings and increasing fragmentation – and even the diminished importance of whiteness – it has too much of a substantial anchor in the distributions of power and wealth and cultural forms of capital to become null and void any time soon. White subjectivity includes a sense of connection to particular forebears and to a particular national narrative. It cannot be replaced by a set of discrete ethnic identifications: these have thinned out for most whites beyond any real meaningfulness, and beyond the possibility of meaningful resuscitation. The history of this nation in European, that is, white, cultures remains central to many people's idea, whether conscious or not, of who we are as a people.

In short, whiteness will continue to exist after it loses its majority status, but it will be living in a country it can no longer so easily dominate.

To be sure, this talk of "whiteness" as an abstract noun can sound strange and in fact be highly misleading, as if whiteness is constituted by some monolithic substance, and as if those who are called white have homogeneous reactions, uniform interests, or a shared culture. Whiteness has none of those things. To speak of whiteness is not to signify a common, separate community, or a uniform psyche shared by all, but a single aspect of one's social identity that operates in concert with other aspects to affect one's formation of self, social relations, and self-understanding. Whiteness is not the most important feature of any individual, though some believe it to be. Nor does it figure the same way across the expanse of trailer parks to the spread of Trump towers. Yet such internal complexities merely make whiteness similar to every other possible way we have to think about and embody our social identities. In this regard, there is no exceptionalism about whiteness.

A View from the Margins

So who am I and where do I personally stand in relation to this topic? My relationship to whiteness is a bit of a complicated story, indicative of the often concealed complexities of whiteness itself.

It is common in writings by African Americans to describe the moment when one "discovers" that one is black, meaning that one discovers one has been placed within a distinct category of people with a particular racial concept that carries negative connotations. Claude Steele

(2010) recounts his own moment on the very first page of his text in social psychology. W.E.B. Du Bois famously recounted his moment of discovery during his New England childhood, when his schoolmates were exchanging "Visiting Day" cards. After a girl "peremptorily, with a glance" refused his card, he sadly discovered how racial identity was dividing the children who were sharing a classroom, rendering it impossible for a white girl to accept his act of friendship. "Then it dawned on me with a certain suddenness that I was different from the others; or like, mayhap, in heart and life and longing, but shut out from their world by a vast veil" (1997/1903, 38) Such moments are related by numerous authors as formative to their developing sense of identity, to their understanding of the social world, and as the beginning of a process by which people come to terms, in one way or another, with the categories of race.

These stories of first awakening to the realities of race are much less common in white memoirs.

My first racial memory was very early. We had just moved away from living in my grandparents' home in Florida; when we would return there for weekly visits, my grandfather would kneel down with a big smile so I could run into his open arms. He would give me a kiss and a nickel or even a quarter. My older sister Vicki hung back. She was still young enough to be hugged and kissed, but somehow she was never treated to my grandparents' affection in the same immoderate way that I was. And I remember at some point along the way beginning to feel a little self-conscious about the disparity, coming to a vague realization that there was something not quite right about the difference in treatment, something that our age difference could not explain.

My sister and I were both "Latin girls," as we were then called. Our father was Panamanian and our mother white, but only Vicki had the beautiful olive skin, black hair, and large dark eyes that made her stand out as so visually distinct in the midst of our mother's Irish family. She was darker, dark enough to be different. I remember thinking about this difference one afternoon when she hurt herself running from the bathroom naked, and I saw her sitting on her bed, crying and rubbing her bruised leg. She had no tan marks, unlike me, just a continuity of brown skin.

Although there are pictures of Vicki being proudly and lovingly held by family members on the US side, she never received the absolute adoration that a first child often generates, unlike in Panama, where she was lavished with typical indulgence. I witnessed all of this, and felt an unarticulated sense of guilt when greeted with deferential delight by my white grandparents. Their love took on a tinge of painfulness. And my grandfather's explosive mockery of dark-skinned faces on television could not but have had disquieting effects on both of us.

Vicki and I would later, gingerly, talk about the disparate treatment we had experienced. My mother confided the difficulty she had in moving in with her parents after she left Panama and separated from my father precisely because she could see their obvious favoritism for me and knew its racial basis. She was desperate to move us out of there. My sister was already having enough of a challenge adjusting to life in the US after our peremptory departure from Panama. It wasn't just that she looked more like my father; it was also that she was four years older, school-age, and spoke only Spanish, while I was younger, lighter, and quicker, at 3, to adapt linguistically. Much later my grandmother confirmed it to me as well: the way she put it was that Vicki was "too different."

Like many younger sisters, I adored my older sister, wanting nothing more than to be in her company. I followed her everywhere, annoying her no end. She was my beautiful older sister, and surely the adoration was natural, but I also felt bonded to her by the common experience of our unique lineage, a sense I later came to understand as being summarily dropped into a white world.

This is my first racial memory. Unlike DuBois, whose experience was of being separated out by a "vast veil" from the world of his classmates, mine was of inclusion within a bifurcated space. I believe this is the more common experience of white people.

This is a book written by a philosopher who grew up in the South in the bosom of a family with whites of different classes, and who has lived through social unrest in close relief as a mixed race person with varied vantage points, within and outside of whiteness.

My identity is quite mixed, or "mixed up" as a hairdresser once told me, given that, as should be clear by now, my nuclear family has some alarming commonalities with Barack Obama's. My mother's family was southern Irish American, while my father was a nonwhite foreigner. Such mixes have been common in Panama since its inception; only more recently is such a trend growing in the United States and elsewhere outside Latin America.

This personal genealogy has given me access to more than one way of being in the world, more than one way of seeing society, more than one way of assessing the rhetorical flourishes used in many topics of public discussion. The political allegiances do not map left to right from my darker to lighter relatives, by any means. There are crypto-fascists among some of my relatives in Panama (followers of the infamous Arnulfistas) and a principled liberalism among some of my white family. There are also white Klansmen and Panamanian Fidelistas. My white family is typical of southern whites who have lived amidst the social changes of the last half-century, affected by the social cataclysms of civil rights, and they have responded to these changes in a variety of ways ranging from *To Kill a Mockingbird* to *Rambo*.

My grandfather, the first generation born away from Ireland, had one year of schooling, started work at the age of 7, held every conceivable job in his life from log-rolling, to work in a steel mill, to haircutting, to – eventually – house-building. He went to night school as an adult to learn to read and write. My grandmother grew up eating meat only when it was caught or trapped or shot. I never saw her wear a real piece of jewelry or any but handmade clothes. My grandparents were short, strong, overweight, highly skilled in numerous practical arts, knowledgeable enough about useful topics to have written multiple books, yet too illiterate to ever read a book. Their everyday clothing was well worn. They were, without a doubt, peasants.

Many folks on the white side of my family were and still are rather poor. By the time my mother was born, her parents were South Carolina sharecroppers and her earliest memory is having a feedsack refashioned for her to hang on her shoulder as she picked cotton in the fields alongside her mother. Picking cotton, my mother says, was not easy; you had to pull the cotton boll off thorny, hard shrubs, generally leaning over in terribly hot sun while you did it. At times while she was growing up, her family was homeless and lived in a railroad car – actually, two railroad cars on an abandoned piece of track, a predictably dark form of living quarters with no facilities of any kind. At other times they lived in the shacks provided for these landless tenants, with no more windows than the railroad cars. The floorboards were wide enough apart that you could feed the chickens who lived underneath the house without having to go outside.

The men in my mother's family were tenant farmers and itinerant laborers, fishermen, bootleggers, truck drivers, and lighthouse keepers. The women planted, canned, sewed, and tended the animals. Their social positionality was as close as whites could get to black people. My mother remembers African Americans in the fields nearby, where they picked cotton, but to say they picked side by side would be an overstatement: she remembers seeing black people in fields appearing to be doing the same work her family was doing, but in different segregated groupings. She also remembers them coming to the edge of a Saturday night pig-roast, hats in hand for the chitlins, the flavorful but least substantial part of the meat. Even at this lowest rung of the economic hierarchy, there was a status difference based on race, and accompanied differences in the activities that one was free to pursue. The status distinction wasn't much compensation. Besides her poor housing, all my mother's clothes were sewn from feedsacks and cast-off materials, and the only meat her family ate was the fish and game they could catch, including possum, bear, and sea turtles.

It was this side of the family that, as I said, I mostly grew up with. I slept in the same bed as my grandmother, with a mattress made from the feathers of birds she had eaten growing up. I have spent some time trying to figure out the complex manifestations of their racism. Their daughter married a brown man (Panamanian, mestizo, mulatto), whom they hesitantly accepted into the family. They took delight in his ability to scale the palm trees in their yard to gather avocados. The fact that he was a foreigner and that he was educated and from a family of schoolteachers (my grandmother's secret aspiration) surely made some difference in their attitude, moderating their reaction. Also, of course, he was brown rather than black, and thus did not "signify" in the pronounced way that southern African Americans would have signified to them as a people with natural inferiority. I would say that, although they were infected with antiblack racism, they didn't have a xenophobic or exclusivist approach to community building, since they lived among so many immigrants for whom English was limited. Foreignness was not unfamiliar.

My parents met in college after my mother reached Florida State University by something of a miracle, one element of which was a scholarship from the Daughters of the Confederacy. She recalls the day her father drove her up to Tallahassee, helping her get settled. His zipper was down on his worn pants the entire day as they interacted with school officials and her new roommates; she was mortified, but he was not the sort of parent that could have born a correction from his daughter, so she weathered her embarrassment in silence.

My father's family was middle class, but he was from an impoverished country in the part of the world sometimes euphemistically referred to as "developing." The Martín's had chickens and fruit trees, and the women of the family were quite skilled in various useful crafts such as intricate sewing and plate painting. Some of my *tias* were dark enough to fear the Klan, and one aunt in particular was convinced that if she ever came to the United States the Klan would meet her as she got off the plane – which gives an indication of the view many people abroad had of the US in those days. In the early 1950s, another of my aunts visited friends for a time in Miami, during which she won a city-wide contest to become "Miss Latin Miami." A small picture of her was in a magazine; the picture of the white "Miss Miami" took a full page. Around the same period, my father, after earning his Master's degree at Florida State, could find no one who would give him a job except to ride a bicycle selling ice-cream.

Although my mother's second marriage made it possible for us to move out from my grandparents' home, we ended up living nearby, and thus I grew up with strong ties to this extended family. My grandparents were kind-hearted people, taking in neighbors' kids from even poorer families for years at a time, and never turning a panhandler away from the door, whether white or black. My grandfather helpfully taught me to distrust preachers and politicians and real estate men, and my grandmother taught me how to garden and to create beauty with seeds and string and used milk cartons. She traveled to Panama in a rickety plane for the event of my birth, and fit right in with my paternal aunts who shared her facilities and interests. She loved Panama and the people she met there, saving every small memento from that trip, as I found after her death. Still, somehow my white grandparents maintained racist views until the day they passed, incoherent as these might have been at times to some of their practices or relationships.

I relate this bit of autobiography here because it is precisely this first-person experience that informs my understanding of the interrelations of class and race. The two cannot be separated, as some suppose, as if poor whites exist outside a racist order, mere dupes or vessels of racism, without direct benefit. My mother's family was not only poor, they were poor white, and both categories are needed to understand their lives, the form of oppression they experienced, the opportunities they had to make a living and (miraculously) get their daughter off to college, as well as the cruel attitudes they could display toward nonwhites. Class reductionist approaches that deny the relevance of whiteness for the white poor do not pay sufficient attention to the psychic benefits of whiteness in racially hierarchical communities, or the social practices of interaction, both formal and informal, that are structured by race. Despite their poverty, they enjoyed a certain freedom of movement, freedom of employment, freedom to vote, freedom to own guns and to hunt, and other freedoms that others did not, and these freedoms made a significant difference to their daily life. In short, both their race and their class are needed to account for their experiences and relationships and thus their formation of identity and subjectivity. As difficult as my white family's lives were, they were not nearly as difficult as those faced by the vast majority of African Americans or Mexicans living in the United States during these decades, who faced not only poverty but also a violent lawlessness that threatened their livelihoods as well as their lives.

To approach the puzzle of what whiteness can become, or how much it can be revised in the future in a nonvanguardist direction, we must come to understand all the things that whiteness has been. And to understand this, we need to have in our minds the poor whites, southern whites, uneducated whites, hardscrabble whites whose trailer existence hardly accounts for much privilege. What are we to say about such whites? Surely whiteness was an important part of the identity of my family; they did not simply have a generic class or regional identity. They were white workers, and white poor, and white southerners, with a distinct experience that was in some respects significantly mediated by race as much as by other social features. And interestingly, this side of the family has not advanced much. One uncle is still too poor to support himself, and lives in a house with a tin roof full of hoarded junk. Other members of the family work in gas stations, as truck drivers, or have joined the military. They avidly watch reality TV. Although the current generation has more education, most still work with their hands. These white lives must be a part of the theorizing we do about the future of whiteness.

The boundaries between racial communities are surely today becoming more porous than they have been in the past. Today my father would probably be able to secure a better job in the United States than riding a bicycle to sell ice cream. As, obviously, have I.

So I come to this project of inquiry with a certain set of background experiences that have given me both insider and outsider sensibilities. I speak about whiteness as someone on the margins of it, though the account herein has been profoundly influenced by the many people I have worked with over the years who, from the very center of whiteness, have been carrying the struggle forward.

I also come not as a sociologist or ethnographer but as a philosopher. The task of philosophers is not to describe the present or chart the trajectories of the past, nor is it to predict the future. We have neither the empirical means nor the methodology at our disposal to glean the facts and produce the explanatory analysis; for that, I have been avidly reading the work of others. The philosopher's task, however, is just as important: to help develop an adequate conceptual repertoire, and to advocate for the future. How should whiteness adapt? How can nonwhites help? What should the meaning of whiteness be in a world where the sad history of unearned white privilege is becoming more often acknowledged as well as repudiated as a legitimate practice?

In reality, whiteness is not simply an identity that emerged from racism and the repression of other groups. The actual complex historical experiences of those marked as white is tremendously varied, and many have known few real privileges. The doomsayers who see only racism in the history and future of whiteness are simply ahistorical essentialists. But there is a real question about what the meaning of whiteness can be outside of a hierarchical framework. What is whiteness, if not supremacy, given the lack of a shared culture across the wide and diverse domain of white people? How can whiteness, in short, become a part of the rainbow of diverse peoples? How can whiteness become bearable?

− 1 −

An Analytic of Whiteness

Social identities in general are a bit of a conundrum, resisted by many. Do we really have to accept these labels? Don't they do more harm than good? How can identity terms of any sort reflect the messy fluidities of human social reality? To get at whiteness, we need first to consider social identity categories in general, and then whiteness in particular. This chapter will try to make some headway in regard to these two tasks.

Whiteness is most obviously a concept, or social construct, and a relatively recent idea in the long expanse of human history. It is not a natural, found object. Differences in skin shades can hardly be classified and neatly categorized with any obvious uniformity, when dark complexioned Greeks, olive-skinned Italians, and pale Scandinavians are grouped together. We have *created* whiteness as a social category of identity. Or somebody has.

Importantly, because racial concepts are social, ideas about particular races can change pretty radically in different social contexts, across time and space, both in terms of the *content* of the ideas and in terms of how this particular content is *valued*. Nothing about our social identities is absolutely fixed.

Our growing sophistication about the variable, context-dependent nature of social categories of identity, together with our growing awareness of the intense damage such divisions have wrought, incline many people today to view social categories as subject to choice. If these categories are socially constructed, it seems to follow that we can choose to un-construct them, so to speak. People around us certainly seem to make conscious choices about how much importance to attach to such categories, and the fact that their choices vary seems to show that this is an arena of free will. Further, it is clear that this process happens not only individually but collectively: by working collectively within communities and societies – using our legislatures and other representative bodies – we can choose whether and how to count races, and how to name, define, and distinguish them, and we can choose whether to base public policy on them. We can enforce their segregation or encourage their integration. We can promote their importance, or try to make it wither away. Or so it would seem.

Two Negative Examples

Societies across the globe are struggling especially with the categories of race and gender, debating whether it is a good idea to acknowledge them, to encourage them, or best to try and ignore them. Consider two stark examples that illustrate the conflicting approaches to identity recently taken in government policy. In the former Yugoslavia, three main ethnic groups – the Serbian, Croatian, and the Bosnian – coexisted *relatively* peacefully for generations (Glenny 1996, 2012; Silber 1997). Although these groups are generally understood to be ethnic rather than racial, when I visited Dubrovnik in 2012 I found many who claimed that there are discernible physical features that can allow one roughly to distinguish them. This means that, in some important respects, these group identities are operating in the way that racial identities do: through visible or otherwise discernible features. "Slavic" identity in general, under which all of these groups are categorized, has a long history of being associated by western Europeans with negative and immutable attributes involving behavioral as well as intellectual capacities, much like racial concepts.

The socialist government in Yugoslavia fell shortly after Tito died in 1980. A tense coalition of communist groups maintained power for 10 years afterward, but when they lost power, several nationalist political parties were quickly formed, dividing the six federated states of the former Yugoslavia strictly along ethnic lines. Parties that used ethnic identity terms in their name – such as the Serbian Democratic Party and the Croatian People's Party – effected a neat conflation of the targeted constituency's ethnic and political identities, as if one's ethnicity determined, and delimited, one's political agenda. Political parties exclusive to specific groups can divide a shared public political culture in a way that is difficult to moderate, replacing a general discussion of the public good with a competition between interest groups defined as oppositional. Such parties institutionalize, in effect, what Cornel West (1994) has called "racial reasoning," in which identity or authenticity checks replace reasoned argument.

In the postcommunist period, stark debates materialized over how this very multiethnic nation should be structured: some supported federalism, others "unitarism," but the situation devolved all too quickly into violence. Adult men were rounded up, sequestered, tortured, and sometimes killed, based only on their ethnic lineage. Women of certain groups were sexually tortured in institutionalized camps, with the conscious aim of demoralizing communities and fracturing their identity alignments.

In the divided areas still today, there are segregated public schools that teach children different accounts of the recent debacle, just as generations of children in the United States learned different versions of the Civil War depending on whether they happened to live north or south of the Mason-Dixon line. Serbian children are taught that their country was engulfed in a civil war spurred on by other groups, Croatian children learn that their people were engaged in a war of self-defense, while Bosnian children are taught that Bosnians suffered a war of genocidal aggression. The segregated educational institutions make it almost impossible for students to develop a comprehensive narrative that might adjudicate between competing claims or develop an adequate explanation for either the development of the war or its legacy. And this seems to be the direct result of treating social categories of identity as determinative and irreducible, with clear-cut definitions and boundaries enforceable by the state.

A second example comes from Rwanda where, by contrast, political and national unity prevails today after the intense period of violence that began in 1994, around the same time as the Balkan War. Rwanda's current government is pursuing a quite different strategy, however, to ameliorate the effects of the war and heal the divisions. Before the war, Rwandan Hutu and Tutsi identities were differentiated by distinctive class positions and accompanying social status, a hierarchy that emerged during the colonial period. The Tutsi were relative newcomers to this area of Africa, and, as Mahmood Mamdani explains: "Through this distinction between alien and indigenous, the Tutsi came to be defined as a race – the Hamitic race – different from the Hutu, who were constructed as indigenous Bantu" (2001, 99). Before independence from colonial rule was won, many Tutsi accepted comprador positions that buffered the white colonizers from the Hutu masses. For this, many were compensated with educational opportunities and material privileges. It is also important to note that Hutu and Tutsi identities, like Yugoslavian ethnicities, are correlated to racialized and generally visible phenotypic features that map their status onto Eurocentric aesthetic hierarchies: the Tutsi are generally taller and lighter skinned.

Given the central role of Hutu and Tutsi identities in mobilizing political and military conflict in the region, and the longstanding class differences and antagonisms between these groups, the current government of Rwanda has endeavored to render these identities politically null in the public domain. Government forms cannot mention them or measure them; official discourses refrain from even noting their existence. In this way, the government hopes to create the nation anew on unified ground.

I want to suggest here that neither of these policies – so diametrically opposed – is plausibly workable. It is highly unlikely that either the segregationist strategy in the former Yugoslavia or the official silence on identity in Rwanda will be effective in avoiding conflict, repairing national trauma, or enhancing solidarity. Schools in the divided nations of the former Yugoslavia are separated from the very populations who not only have a different political orientation, but important experiences necessary for a full understanding of the actions taken by their own leadership during the war. Fairytales with comforting or exculpatory historical narratives will not be challenged. The Rwandan government is similarly attempting to transcend traumatic historical events by a kind of non-engagement. In truth, Hutu and Tutsi identities continue to affect social interactions, whether recognized by the government or not. These identities with longstanding tensions now have the added intensity of traumatic memories of atrocity, of victimization, and, no less traumatically, of the culpability for atrocities. To amass them together asks people, as Sonia Sikka points out, "to identify themselves with groups which... committed wrongs against their proximate ancestors. For most people, such self-identification is, at a psychological level, simply impossible" (2004, 348). Censoring identity talk only impedes the project of reassessing identities and reimagining their possible interrelationships. The meanings of identities are fluid, but segregation and silence hinder the process in which the meanings of identities may be understood more comprehensively and accurately, and hence transformed.

Here, then, we have opposing strategies both of which offer negative case studies. In the former Yugoslavia, the push to separate ethnic identities continues, as new Serbian ethnic studies programs are developed replete with newly constructed literary canons and language instruction, even though most believe that Serbian and Croatian constitute dialects, not full languages. This cultural nationalism is fueled by political mobilization. In Rwanda, Mamdani suggests that the "attainment of self-enlightenment by guilty majorities has been a painfully gradual process" (2001, 279). Certainly, the effort to make identities less visible makes it difficult to assess the real effects of the past on the present.

People in the United States should in no way feel superior to these beleaguered regions in terms of our ability to come to terms with social diversity or the traumas of history. Political discourse in the United States operates on the surface a bit like Rwanda even while constituencies pursue what they take to be their racial interests in a fashion closer to the former Yugolsavia. "Contemporary American race talk," as Jack Turner bluntly asserts, "is stagnant" (2012, x). It is overly simplistic and dominated by a policy of avoidance of the role that race has played in the nation's founding. In 2015, the first ever museum dedicated to slavery will be opened in the United States, a full century and a half after its abolition (Amsden 2015). Legally sanctioned Jim Crow has given way to an insidious social violence in which social welfare, union rights, wages, and even worker safety regulations are slashed for the lower stratum of the workforce, a stratum well known for its racial diversity. Race profoundly affects employment, imprisonment, and home ownership, and yet there continues to be tension around causal attributions that name race as a factor in social inequity, and charges of discrimination are derided as a "politics of victimhood." Among whites of many political persuasions, talk of race generates awkwardness, a discomfort perhaps motivated by the idea that, if we talk about the race of others, they may talk about our race as well.

So, in the safe space of this book, let's talk about whiteness. The first task is to talk about social identities in general. Let's agree, at least for now, that neither the former Yugoslavia nor Rwanda has a plausible approach: identities are neither fixed and all-determining, nor are they eliminable by government policy. So if neither approach makes sense, what approach would?

Let's begin with a general account of social identity categories, and then move to the particularity of whiteness as a category today. The goal of improving on the accounts of identity playing out in Rwanda and the former Yugoslavia may well seem like a low bar, but consideration of these examples may give us confidence to forge ahead.

A more *realistic* account of identity, I'll argue, would be a *realist* view that understands identities to be significant aspects of the social world and of our lived sense of who we are and how we are positioned in the immediate social environs in which we live and work. Government policies can play a large role, but not an absolutely determinative one. Part of this more realist view will involve an understanding that the categories of race and ethnicity are not always easily separable, no matter how much academics or policymakers have wanted to parse the distinction. In the real world, ethnic groups are often racialized, and racialized groups are clearly noticeable as we move through social spaces, whether they are allowed on government forms or not. The racial diversity, or lack thereof, of our immediate social space can profoundly affect how relaxed, or how fearful, we are. Even though races are not found objects, they cannot be so easily legislated away or wished out of existence.

What Social Identities Are

If we try a realistic approach to how social categories of identity operate in our lives, it is clear that we cannot always choose when our identities are politically salient, or how they are salient, or how much. This has often been recognized as true for those whose social identities are the occasion for discrimination and violence, but it is equally true for those whose identities are not social liabilities, such as whites. There is a limit to how much individuals can control their social environment, and even groups cannot control how a given group identity will be seen in the larger society. I cannot decisively control the way others interpret my actions, nor can I always predict the effects of my actions.

Let us be clear on this point: the *political* salience of identities is dependent on their *social* salience. That is, identities can be politically mobilized only when what is being invoked has some connection to our social lives, that is, our lives in society, however partial and perhaps distorted that invocation is. What does it mean for an identity to be socially salient?

I will argue that, in reality, social identity categories such as race and ethnic identities retain the social salience that they do because they are (1) explanatory, (2) an aspect of our material existence, (3) a feature of collective or group subjectivity, and (4) the necessary effect, at least in some cases, of historical experiences. When an identity term, such as whiteness, fulfills these four conditions, then the use of the identity term, and the belief in its existence, cannot be chalked up to an ideological obfuscation of reality. I will briefly describe each of these claims.

(1) Social identities are explanatory in the sense that they help to explain the social world as well as our own individual experiences. They can explain, for example, some of the reactions we experience, both positive and negative, from the people around us. In this sense, we might think of social identity categories as "small theories" by which we navigate our social worlds, as Satya Mohanty has argued. Mohanty (1997) takes identity terms as providing narratives that explain the links between group historical memory and individual contemporary experience, creating unifying frames that provide a descriptive purchase on the patterns of social interaction and the hierarchies of status and distribution that we see around us every day. In this

sense, identity terms are not mere historical holdovers of oppression, or ideological claims, but explanatory terms that help us to make sense of what we experience as well as to comprehend larger historical events.

Mohanty holds that there is an important advantage to thinking of social identities as "small theories" in this way: it helps us more readily to understand them to be social constructions rather than natural phenomena. It is true that theories can be generated about natural as well as social phenomena, from the movements of planets to the movements of capital. But theories are themselves always fallible social constructions generated out of specific aims and conditions. This is what philosophers of science mean when they say that theories are always situated: they are produced for certain purposes, for example, to provide an explanation that will establish blame, or, alternatively, help us control our environment. Thus, all theories have a limited explanatory reach or scope of application; no theory can explain everything.

Theories can play multiple roles, from generating predictions and causal laws based on natural processes, to charting correlations. But most generally, theories are attempts at explanation. Explanation itself can take various forms, not simply involving causal laws with predictive capacity, but also in terms of the historical formation of a phenomenon, its genealogy, how it is reproduced or reinforced, what social effects it has, and thus, in general, how it fits relationally within a social context. The explanatory value and predictive capacity of theories are often contextually dependent in regard to natural phenomena, but also in regard to social kinds of things. Our ability to explain the ways in which whiteness operates will certainly depend on the particularities of context. If we understand identity terms as theories in this way, we will take them to be fallible or revisable, and, most importantly, contextually dependent and limited in their explanatory reach.

Once we begin to understand identities as "small theories," we can subject them to a kind of empirical test for adequacy, asking whether in fact they explain what they purport to explain, or whether they conceal and distort more than they reveal. We might ask, does whiteness actually *explain* cross-class allegiances among white people, or does it divert our attention from better explanations? Does the identity category of Latino have much explanatory value given the variety of ethnic, national, and racial groups it is meant to contain? By subjecting identity categories to empirical tests in this way, we can explore their empirical adequacy and explanatory value. We can point out what the category "whiteness" does and does not explain, and in some cases we can begin to revise and reformulate identity concepts to develop more adequate terms. We can also resist the biological notions of race that racist essentialists use to explain economic success, even while retaining the historical and social notions of race that play a role in the persistence of inequality.

The important idea here is that the persistence and influence of identity categories is related to their explanatory capacity. We hold onto them not because we are deluded (at least, not in every case) but because they are *useful*. Racial identity concepts help us to make sense of our world, but, like other theoretical constructs, they can also at times lead us astray, especially if we take them too literally, or as infallible, absolute, and unalterable. The validity of identity terms is an effect of their explanatory utility, and this means that if they become more hindrance than help, we can set them aside. But as long as they remain useful, they will be used.

(2) Social identities are also material practices. The metaphor used above about how identity categories help us to "navigate our world" should signify quite literally the material practice in which we learn how to interact with others and interpret what people say and do. Related to the material practice of identity is the fact that identities are often, though not always, *visible* features of our material social worlds, producing a kind of visual registry organizing the interactions in social spaces. Status

correlates to how much people smile, touch, pay attention to and look directly at one another, and follow one's conversational cues, and social identities are generally status determinants. The idea of the visible here is an important one, but the idea of material, perceptible difference obviously extends far beyond sight to every other perceptual sensibility, from hearing to touch.

In this way, identities should not be thought of merely as a discursive or linguistic overlay on top of materially instantiated differences, but as a meaningful (or meaning-laden) organization of the phenomenologically accessible material world. A simpler way of saying this is that identities are not mere talk but an aspect of our material environment.

The material or perceptible basis of identity categories does not in and of itself determine the meaning and significance we attach to any given features, no matter how pronounced. That is, extreme differences, such as height or size or powerful smells, do not automatically determine that we will respond with animosity or attraction, or that we will feel a comparative superiority or inferiority, or even that we will take the extreme difference to be germane to much of anything. Here, culturally specific meaning-systems play the determining role in conferring *status* differences on *perceptible* differences. By saying that identities are material, the point is not that their meaning or correlate status is entirely determined by their materiality, but to counsel against the idea that identities are illusions or mere figments of our ideologically befuddled imagination.

Of course, the way in which we take note of differences can be learned; the "obviousness" of some differences is dependent on early training to pick out and focus on specific kinds of attributes. Many of the perceptual practices by which we learn to tell the "difference" between, for example, an Arab or an Italian are hardly natural or automatic; crossing contexts, one can find one's own identity perceived quite differently and entirely misperceived. This is what has given rise to jokes about how developed one's "gay-dar" or "jew-dar" is. Clueless perceivers who have not been inculcated with local perceptual practices (or group-specific practices) are the stuff of comedy. But the fact that one must *learn* a set of skills to know which characteristics are relevant, as well as the important lines of demarcation between groups, does not mean that what we are perceiving is imaginary or reducible to ideology. Much has been made of the fact that eye color signifies less intensely in the United States than skin color, sometimes to suggest that the material differences count for nothing and all that matters is the meanings we attach to them. The actor Michael Ealy's green eyes do little to change the fact that he is restricted to roles for African Americans. Yet, besides the fact that in some parts of the world eye color can actually count quite a lot (see, for example, Candelaria 2007), it is a mistake to treat the perceptible features of identity as if these were mere epiphenomena of discourse that play no role in the formations of meaning. It is undoubtedly true that in a European-dominated aesthetic field we are trained to perceive and overemphasize small differences or physical aspects that should be trivial, but what we are perceiving is not an illusion in and of itself. Children may vary in which visible or otherwise perceptible cues they focus on, but from very early ages they learn to navigate their worlds by such differences. There is plenty of research to show how learned this process is: age and gender may trump race in small children's memories, thus indicating what categories have greater social importance in their given context. Lawrence Hirschfeld's work, for example, shows that the perception of racial differences may require *more* learning than the perception of age (Hirschfeld 1996). Yet the fact that we learn how to organize and interpret material differences, as well as which ones to pick out as the most socially relevant, does not prove that social relations could *or should* operate without taking note of differences, or that all such differences *are only* perceptible as the result of learned practice. As Patricia Williams (1997) argues, promoting "colorblindness" or attempting to ignore entirely the distinctiveness of bodily types and appearances are simply unrealistic proposals that will mask, rather than overcome, the practices of racism. Even if we take as a goal diminishing the meaningfulness of racialized physical attributes, it is simply untrue that attempting to ignore such attributes today will realize the dream. In fact, spreading the lie that it is possible to ignore entirely such racialized differences helps to conceal racism.

A better approach is to learn to look at these visible differences differently, to see more comprehensively and more accurately. Learning to see more perceptively will undoubtedly break down the false binaries often drawn between identities, exposing the heterogeneity within every group and the commonalities across groups. But this will not eliminate the visible difference. As Pat Parker (1999) put it in her famous poem, "For the White Person Who Wants to Know How To Be My Friend":

The first thing you do is forget that I'm black.
Second, you must never forget that I'm black.

Color-blindness counsels against the latter, while racism makes the former impossible. But Parker's dictum makes perfect sense: of course our identities are important features of who we are, not something to "overlook." Just as important, they are not all of who we are.

To say that identities are material is not only to mark the perceptible physical correlates of identity, but to draw attention to our lived environments, in which public culture continues to present a white dominant world. In private colleges, one often teaches or presents lectures in rooms full of richly painted portraits of past presidents or rich benefactors, all white. The various government offices, from police stations to motor vehicle departments, hang pictures of presidents, governors, mayors, and commissioners, mostly a uniform set. From the statuary that fills our public parks to religious imagery, the shared material environment of daily life portrays a white world. Embodied images are, of course, unnecessary to create this atmosphere: street and town names, from Harrisburg to Onondaga to Saint Augustine, can also signify identity, commemorating a European dominance and colonial past without critique. This is the backdrop of everyday life.

(3) Social identities are also correlated to existing organizations of social practices, including the ways we learn to perceive one another. Patterns of perceptual attunement – or what we are likely to notice, what we foreground, and what exists only in the background – are in some measure connected to our association with various groups (Monahan 2010). Our sensitivity to slight often varies by group identity, leading to charges of "oversensitivity" by those who do not share the same perceptual attunements. Some whites see antiwhite prejudice looming whenever histories of racism come up for discussion; unable to focus on what is happening to the oppressed groups, they foreground every potential reference to whites or European Americans and display extreme sensitivity to slights, real or imagined (Smith 1994).

The perception of prejudice is in general a judgment call, requiring an interpretation of a particular interaction. And judgment is affected by our perceptual attunements as well as our baseline knowledge, or what we already know or believe. We use our baseline knowledge to try to make sense of new experiences – but this too is in some measure connected to our socialization as a member of various groups. The founder of social psychology, George Herbert Mead, pointed out that we are all born into an already existing and finely regulated system of shared meanings. This system organizes our self-consciousness, as he famously put it, "from the outside in" (see Alcoff 2006, 117ff). There is no fully formed self prior to our absorption in a system of social meanings. Importantly, Mead's view is not that there is a Big Brother who forces us to perceive in a certain way, but that the individual gains an understanding of the meaningful world and his or her place within it in the same way that fans at a sports game come to perceive the events on the field. Fans react not simply to sheer athletic skill, but to the way that skill is deployed, or not, in light of the rules of the game. A great run will get cheers or jeers depending entirely on whether the player is running in the right direction. We could no more understand the reactions of fans without reference to the rules of the game than we can understand political actors as mere individuals operating independently of collectively shared meanings.

When I attend baseball or football games with my partner, it is almost as if we are attending different events. He knows the history of the teams, the stakes of this particular game, the statistics of every player, the dispositions of the coach. He often chats away with people seated around us using a shorthand I can only guess at. His attention is riveted; mine tends to wander. He knows where to look and whom to watch, while I routinely lose the train of events. He has a skill born of a lifetime of sports, imbricated with affective components based on memories of going to games with his grandfather and playing such games as a kid. My distraction and boredom are also born of a childhood in which sports knowledge was never shared. I also get aggravated by the cheerleaders' costumes and dance steps, by the macho fans screaming insults at young guys who make mistakes on the field, and by the fact that such huge quantities of people are focused on men at play in a way they never focus on women. We have different perceptual attunements, baseline knowledges, foregrounds and backgrounds, and affective experiences. I like it when he provides color commentary for my benefit, explaining what he is seeing on the field, its layered meanings and significance. I enjoy entering into his world. But even so, my world never disappears from sight; I still get aggravated by the cheerleaders.

Our social identities are related in obvious ways to the different experiences we have of sporting events, but the relation is obviously complicated. Many women enjoy sports; many men do not. I could no doubt school myself on the relevant system of meanings, though I could never replicate the rich trove of memories my partner has. My partner is also aggravated by the sexism on display in the cheerleaders' costumes and movements, though his aggravation takes the form of embarrassment since he knows it is intended for his benefit and he wants no part of it. He is also aggravated by macho fans and the general political problems with major league sports, but he has so many positive connections to the game that his enjoyment is not as diminished as mine. Some elements of these perceptual practices, then, can be the result of conscious choices and commitments, while others are arbitrary effects of our upbringing.

Social identities, then, are sometimes correlated to the systems of collective meaning we happen to be immersed within, in which emotion-laden memories, perceptual attunements, and intelligible reasons operate within a shared communal organization that affects our practices of interpretation and judgment, as well as our affective responses (Markus and Moya 2010). As I said, social identities do not by themselves determine such outcomes – women can be sports fans, men can become quite knowledgeable about social signs of sexism – but there are obvious connections at times between the way we perceive and judge and experience an event and who we are. In some cases this means we simply notice different elements, but in other cases this can mean that we might be seriously ignorant about the meaning and significance of events we witness. In some cases such differences produce innocuous differences of interpretation, while in others such differences can impair our perception of the truth. Part of what it means to have a social identity, then, is to have one's self formed within a collective system of meanings that bears elements of that identity.

(4) As this last point reveals, ultimately, social categories of identity are the product of history. This is especially true of racial and ethnic identities, whose terms evolve from

group-related historical events. Another way to say this is that social identities are the residues of history that make up part of the context within which we must fashion ways of being in the world. The influential British cultural theorist Stuart Hall writes that "identities are the names we give to the different ways we are positioned by, and position ourselves within the narratives of the past" (1990, 225). This formulation retains an individual agency within an account that gives history its due.

History organizes the present through its effects on our emotional responses and the traumatic or inspiring memories of our ancestors' struggles. History also affects the norms that engender our habits of practice, the assumptions we make, and the forms of interaction and behavior that we find natural or that we engage in automatically. And of course there is a powerful historical legacy from the ways in which resources were distributed in the past that continues to produce status differentiations today, as well as institutions and institutional practices that prescribe and proscribe our behavior.

Danielle Allen (2004) nicely characterizes these effects as "history's gravity." She vividly describes the "congealed distrust" and "deep rules" that organized the modes of interaction between whites and blacks during the civil rights movement of the twentieth century, a movement she calls a civil war. To say that a girl in a black and white dress attending her first day of school met a mob threatening to kill her just for being there makes no sense until we know it was Little Rock, Arkansas in 1957, the girl was African American, and the mob white. Our ability for a free and engaged responsiveness to new events, such as the ability to respond to the profound event of widespread black resistance to Jim Crow, must work within and against the habits of identity-based interaction into which we are inculcated from birth.

As a child I listened to white family members describe black political resistance as dangerous and a form of criminal activity, and as instigated by outsiders whose moral language concealed other less-than-moral motives. This was an interpretation of events overdetermined by my relatives' own histories and upbringing. History doesn't excuse us, but it explains the conditions in which the interpretive process is occurring: what concepts I have at my disposal, how I am positioned vis-à-vis the "deep rules" of my milieu, and, most importantly, what of my own history is at stake as I try to make sense of new events. Today I watch the privileged white children of the upper East Side in New York City where I work verbally abuse their nonwhite nannies on the street – pre-school-age children! – and I wonder at the alarming persistence of these old modes of interaction, based all too obviously in the persistent patterns of service employment rooted in slavery and colonialism. The history of organizing service work via racial difference reaches its noxious tentacles into the present. Clearly, such modes of disrespectful interaction as I witness today will continue, while economic and social roles provide a foundation for them. It is our shared histories, global and local, that have overdetermined the ways in which the labor market continues to be organized by our identities, and the ways in which we continue to perceive and judge each other. Thus are our identities, or aspects of them, a historical residue.

Social identity categories that denote ethnicity, nationality, race, and religion – such as Puerto Rican, or Jewish, or Italian American, or white – connect individuals to group histories with which they have some genealogical connection, however complex this connection may be. In most people's everyday understanding in the United States, what it means if I say that I am Irish or Panamanian is simply that I have one or two parents who are Irish or Panamanian. This understanding may or may not continue to hold if I was adopted, if it was not my parents but my great-grandparents who were Irish, if the family continues many or few of the cultural practices associated with those ethnic identities, and so on.

But despite the complexities in any given individual's life, a genealogical connection often produces in those individuals a set of affective and cognitive responses to specific events, stories, or narratives that are somewhat different from others – causing them to foreground what others may overlook, and to experience an emotional reaction in some cases that others may not share. I don't really appreciate jokes about drunken uncouth Irishmen, but the stereotypes about the Irish disposition to brawl remind me of family stories about my uncles' violent fights that provide some discomfiting confirmation. Like a lot of people from small countries or minority ethnicities, I know the name of every Panamanian who plays on a major sports team in the US, and I flinch internally at the negative comments boxing fans typically make about the legendary Panamanian fighter Roberto Duran for quitting in the middle of his 1981 bout with Sugar Ray Leonard. More significantly, every Panamanian I know (over the age of 30 or thereabouts), whether they are now living in Panama or in Brooklyn, has a strong opinion about, and emotional reaction toward, the US invasion of their country in 1989. There is a great deal of political disagreement, yet our shared national identity provides a lens through which we view US foreign policy and US government pronouncements about a variety of issues concerning Latin American countries.

Identities also have obvious impact on the tenor of personal interaction, generating friendliness, trust, or the reverse. I have discovered that the decal of a Panamanian flag on the back of my VW routinely generates friendly smiles from parking-lot attendants all over Manhattan. Upon seeing the decal, people have rolled down their windows at stoplights to chat with me about where in Panama they are from. One's social identities (for everyone has a multiple set, not just mixed folks such as myself) do not necessarily affect *most* of what we notice and foreground in normal everyday circumstances, but it may nonetheless affect how we respond to others, as well as how we respond to a wide range of news stories, movies, and so on. In this way it affects who we are.

The genealogies of identity terms such as "black" and "white" and "mestizo" have all now been traced with some accuracy to complex colonial histories. The large events of modern, postconquest history – such as slavery, genocide, the annexation of massive amounts of land, the economically or politically motivated diasporas of numerous peoples, and of course numerous wars – played central roles in the formation and transformations of identity as well as the establishment of status and hierarchy, and they also played a role in the development of specific collective cultural traditions and rituals that people created in order to survive, remember, and make sense of such cataclysmic events.

Social categories of identity are not simply foisted on us from above, dependent on state recognition, but organically produced out of such historical events.

Nonetheless, such macro events underdetermine our individual responses and political interpretations of their meaningfulness in our lives. It is obvious that different individuals will interpret and respond to the same event quite differently, and there will be contestation over the practices and official interpretations enshrined in group rituals that mark national and ethnic identities. The conceptual repertoire available for our interpretative and explanatory work is, in a sense, arbitrary, arising from what Michel Foucault wittily named our "historical *a priori*" that set the terms of intelligibility and coherence. Nonetheless, large events of history demand interpretation, and their erasure or minimizing requires quite a bit of work and regular vigilance. Those most adversely impacted by such events cannot so easily ignore them, but must either struggle to make sense of our histories or work vigilantly to cover over the evidence of their effects on our lives.

One way to understand this complex role of history in relation to identity is to make use of Hans-Georg

Gadamer's (1991/1960) concept of the hermeneutic horizon. This is the idea of an interpretive horizon that operates as a backdrop and orienting perspective from which individuals make sense of new events. Gadamer conceptualizes our horizon as a location from which we look out at the world, but it also has content. It is not simply a neutral place but a substantive outlook containing a variety of elements very specific to us as individuals. Our horizon is also open and dynamic, constantly accumulating new elements, sometimes motivating the reinterpretation of existing elements.

This concept of the horizon helps us to capture the background, framing assumptions we bring with us to perception and to the effort of understanding. Some of the content of our horizons will be group-related, and thus experienced by all those who share a social identity, such as the trauma of dislocation or slavery, the perpetual encounter with racist representations, or the memories of collective violence. The horizon does not determine how particular individuals will interpret such shared experiences. But we cannot control with simple volition our affective responses to events that affected our forebears, or the way in which such responses orient our perceptions, setting them in the foreground, mobilizing our sympathies, our fears, or our hatreds.

To argue for the importance of history in this way may seem to downplay the role of interpretation, or the fact that no historical event carries its determinate political meaning on its back, as it were, but can be endlessly interpreted and assessed anew. Group identity itself is the product of interpretive work. My feelings of connection to the history of a particular group is dependent on how the events are understood. I have two great-grandfathers who fought for the Confederacy: do I sympathize with the extreme difficulty of their experience as whites, as southerners facing "northern aggression" and superior arms, as poor men forced or bamboozled by landowners to conscript, or do I condemn their armed defense of a slave system? Differences of historical interpretation will affect how far my expansive imaginative sympathies may be able to travel. But there is a kind of "raw material" in our histories and lineages that can operate in surprisingly powerful ways, as evidenced when one finds out later in life a lineage that causes new empathies, or angers, to arise, or when one revises one's interpretation so that a villain becomes a victim. Felt connections are the product of mediated processes of interpretation, and yet they are not simply ours to choose or to interpret out of existence.

These four realist elements provide a way to think about the realistic dimensions of social identity categories that limit the elasticity of our individual power of choice as well as the effectiveness of political attempts to manipulate us or force changes, whether progressive or regressive. As long as identity terms offer explanations of our social world, they will continue to be useful, and used. They are ways of naming aspects of our interpretive horizons, likely perceptual attunements, and connections to history. Identities are the result of social rather than natural processes, and yet they emerge organically from these realist elements. Thus, the efforts to eliminate or minimize social categories of identity may fail, or in fact undermine, our capacity to explain our surroundings, our experiences, and our own practices, as well as the practices of others. The attempt by states (or cultural theorists) to alter identity terms will need to take these desiderata into account.

This *realist approach to social identity* will be used throughout the following account of whiteness, a very particular form of identity. In the remainder of this chapter, I will address the key issues that may appear to preemptively disable an account of white identity: the issue of "race" itself as a specious category, the important issue of class, and the problem of, as one might say, the "one and the many," or the lack of a unifying essence that can provide unity across difference. After discussing these issues, I will turn to the question of what is it we are talking about when we talk about whiteness? This is a different question from the question of what *grounds* identity claims, or what justifies our belief that they are real, as I just discussed via the four points above. Rather, it is a question about the referent of the concept of "whiteness" or "white identity."

The History of "Race"

As a category of social identity, race is a beleaguered term. The concept has only emerged in the modern period, and from the very beginning developed under a cloud of willfully mistaken ideas about putative biological essences (Harding 1993). The variety within any given racialized group provided plenty of evidence, even before the genomic facts became known, that race is not a sufficient cause of anything important such as behavior or intelligence or moral dispositions. Yet scientists throughout the nineteenth century, including the revered Louis Agassiz, as well as Darwin, Cuvier, Morton, and Buffon, overlooked countervailing evidence, shoddily produced classification tables of human types based on appearance, and mangled IQ tests to suggest that they reveal permanent capacities (Gould 1996).

By the 1990s, biologists and anthropologists – the two disciplines that had played the most troubling role in the proliferation of ideas about race – reached a consensus that the concept did not refer to anything physiologically or biologically real. DNA testing showed that there is much more genetic variance within than across racial groups. We can statistically tabulate many patterns involving group identities, but, given the newly reliable scientific evidence, we now understand that what we are tracking are not biologically caused phenomena, but socially caused factors. Some thought that even if we redefine race as a social kind rather than a biological kind, this would be problematic given the history of the concept. Kwame Anthony Appiah (1992) argued that race continued to imply biology, and a continued use of the term would simply perpetuate the muddle. Others such as Paul Gilroy (2000) argued that the concept's continued use could only bode ill for efforts toward social justice.

Since that time, two interesting developments have emerged, one in regard to the science debates and another in regard to the social definitions of race. First, many biologists and philosophers of biology have changed their mind about the full-on speciousness of the category. Population geneticists have found a way to correlate socially recognized categories of race not to genes or genetically related dispositions, but to histories of population groups (Andreasen 1998; Kitcher 2007; Spencer 2012). In other words, one can use's one racial identity to track the likely continental home of one's ancestors, as one can on the TV show *Finding Your Roots*. Others use what is called "junk DNA" – non-explanatory DNA – to fashion a biological category of race (Pierce 2014). Importantly, these new methods of giving a biological content to the social categories of race do not produce predictions or explanations as the old theories claimed to do, so debate continues over their scientific utility. Meanwhile, the medical sciences have begun to push race-specific pharmacological commodities big time. Here, some excellent young philosophers of science are playing a useful role in debunking the complicated methodologies bolstering these claims, pointing out, for example, that the evidence nowhere establishes discreteness or uniqueness – that is, that all and only black males respond to a given heart medication (Maglo 2010, 2011). Given this complexity, physicians need to continue to fashion treatments based on individual history rather than jumping to group-based conclusions.

While the science debate over race has been reinvigorated with these new developments, another development has emerged in the social theory literature since the 1990s. Denying that the category of race is a social construct is analogous to denying climate change, as David Theo Goldberg (2014) insists. But denying the reality of race because it has a social and historical rather than a biological genealogy is just as foolish, as Goldberg also argues. Michael Omi and Howard Winant (1994) have produced a particularly compelling concept of "racial formation" as a way to talk about racial identities that foregrounds their dynamic and flexible, socially embedded character. Using a broadly Foucauldian approach, like Goldberg, they explore the processes of racial formation as a bottom-up/top-down dialectic, in which social movements of resistance, and not just state institutions, play a substantial role. Their concept of racial formation makes it possible to study the significance of race without further contributing to the specious assumptions about its naturalism. Critical race studies have mostly followed this approach: to study race as a moving target. There are varied projects among critical race theorists, with some aiming for a future without race and others leaving that particular door open. But what unites this trend is the determination to critique racial projects and racial discourses even as race is, at the same time, understood to be, at least for now, quite real. (See e.g. Carter 2000; Fine et al. 1997; Hartigan 1997; Ingram 2005.)

The use of race categories in this book follows this general approach of critical race theory. The theory of social identities I offer is meant to flesh out our understanding of how social dynamics form races, racialized groups, and racial identities, and not just racial ideas. As far as the science debates go, while a bit skeptical, I also follow with interest the ongoing discussions. The main question for this side of the scholarship is whether such a population-based definition of race adds anything substantial to our understanding of how race works in society and politics. The critical race approach that emphasizes race as fundamentally social has a more obvious and immediate pay-off.

Ethnicity cannot replace race, as I have argued elsewhere and will reiterate here in regard to whiteness (Alcoff 2006, 2009; see also Hattam 2007). Ostensibly, ethnic categories denote chosen cultural groupings with shared lineage, but the focus is less on lineage and phenotype than on volitional commitments and practices. Hence, historically, ethnicity is distinguished from race as culture is from biology. This historical demarcation does not reflect the real-world way of speaking, in which ethnic terms slide over into racial terms all the time. "African American" gets used interchangeably with "black" in many parts of the US, thus grouping together Caribbean and African immigrants and once again rendering what is an apparent ethnic term – "African American" – a racial term. The concept "Latino" likewise ostensibly denotes an uber-ethnicity, and yet the racialization of Latinos is evident in every right-wing political discussion: we are all alike, and most of what we are is negative. If we understand the meaning of terms to track their actual use in living speech, as I will argue in Chapter 2, then the use of ethnic terms often reveals a synonymy with race. This complicates any strategy of replacing race with ethnicity.

I do not take whiteness to refer to a biological category, or a genetic grouping. Rather, whiteness is a social kind distinguishable from specific ethnic or national identities even if it is used to refer to an amalgam of specific ethnicities that share a lineage based in Europe. If we drop the term whiteness, we will miss the proverbial elephant, and one of the most important explanatory variables for social dynamics of labor and material distribution.

Beyond the developments in critical race theory, there has more recently emerged a constellation of social theory sometimes called "decolonial studies" (Quijano 2008; Grosfoguel et al. 2005). This work locates the development of racial formations within a modern colonial world framework dating from the conquest of the "new world," so-called. From Columbus's journals forward we can follow the history of a racialized representation of labor, or what Anibal Quijano calls the "coloniality of power," a phrase meant to signify the colonial history embedded in the way in which political, economic, and social power is organized, and in which, for example, labor groups are divided up and organized, subjecting some to perpetual lawn service while others are given a computer and placed in a cubicle. The racialization of the labor market, which one can observe in any hospital, nursing home, factory, university, or corporation, developed prior to capitalism in colonial conquest. This is the system we are still living with today, in which black people from the Caribbean have better chances on the job market than African Americans, and lighter skinned Latinos fare better than those with more obvious indigenous features. The racial segmentation of labor has organized capital flows since the beginning of modernity in a way few leftists have come to terms with.

Class

Which brings us to the topic of class. The idea that we should focus on class rather than race gains momentum from a consideration of how white workers have been misled to believe in an imagined race solidarity over the real prospects of class solidarity. Race and racism persistently obscure economic realities, such as when the 2008 real estate debacle and foreclosure epidemic was blamed on African Americans and Latinos for pursuing mortgages they could not afford, invoking racist stereotypes about their financial recklessness, rather than on the (largely white-owned) banks that profited enormously from such lending practices.

However, the concept of class itself needs some analysis. Both classical economics and Marxist concepts of class developed in and for a European context, with typically Eurocentric deficiencies given the theorist's ignorance about economic practices and political histories outside Europe. Marx defined class in terms of one's role in the production of capitalist commodities, or, in other words, one's relationship to capital. This is not easily transposable to other sorts of economic configurations, such as slavery or conscripted labor, or roles defined in terms of caste or feudal relations or the *latifundias* and *gamonales* instituted in colonized countries. The native peoples owned land, even as recognized by the state, and yet could be forcibly conscripted into the mines because of their racial identity, a fate that Marx's analysis does not explain. To have one's labor role based on one's identity was a feudal practice by Marx's definition, and to explain the fact that this practice continues today even in late capitalism requires a theoretical subterfuge if one wants to stay within Marxist terminology. It is understandable, then, that the gendered and racialized nature of labor has been consistently underplayed in the Marxist tradition, since theorists have found it difficult to adapt Marxism to the realities of a labor market organized and segmented in terms of racial and gendered groups. To call for a focus on class, then, rather than race and gender, is to call for a diminution if not erasure of the latter's importance.

It is critical to refuse these either/or proposals and insist on developing integrated analyses. I would argue that race, in the sense just defined as an identity formation owing its emergence to new world colonialism, has carried since its inception an embedded *economic* meaning. The attributes used to define racial *types* were originally a set of criteria for exploitation: what kind of work could the Native peoples be made to do? What kind of skills might Africans bring? Under what conditions would Asian labor remain docile? These were the questions that started the ball rolling on racial concepts. Interestingly, labor resistance has been consistently intertwined with specific identity formations that either hindered organization or grounded it. The greatest revolutions in the western hemisphere – in Haiti and in Mexico – were formulated in racial terms, as African slaves against their white masters, and as an alliance of mestizos and Indians, rather than generic workers and peasants, against the criollos. Every liberatory theorist in Latin America, from Simón Bolívar to José Martí to José Carlos Mariátegui, has had to make racial identities a centerpiece of their analysis, not an afterthought. The complex economic developments of North America throughout the modern period, and the shifting racial and ethnic segmentations of labor, have much more in common with the rest of this hemisphere than they do with Europe. But these issues are as global as the reach of colonial and settler states (McCarthy 2009).

Racial formations have a materiality beyond volitional self-ascription, organizing labor resources and all but determining one's position as unskilled, semiskilled, manual laborer, service worker, craftsman, manager, and so on (Barrera 1979). As Omi and Winant's (1994) term "racial formation" is intended to signify, this materiality is always in transition. Throughout the United States today, the materiality of race is in major transition as science, technology, engineering, and mathematics (STEM) fields make efforts to diversify and the possibility of a truly multiracial professional-managerial class comes into view (Alba 2009). And yet, the labor force remains obviously segmented around racial identities. Diversification in the upper-middle strata is not translating into an eradication of the racial configuration of the broad bottom. The back of the house is still most often black and brown.

When I was in my early twenties I worked for a time as a seamstress in a large shirt factory outside Atlanta, one of the largest unionized shirt factories in the world. I was given a sewing test and then assigned a position in the relatively easy collars department. The 1,500 workers in the plant, almost all women, were organized by race and gender to an extent that one could not overlook: floor sweepers and cleaners were African American men, cutters were white men, the more taxing composition jobs (such as those that involved having a spray of steam in a worker's face eight hours a day) were done entirely by African American women, and the seamstress jobs were primarily white women with a scattering of African American women, Filipinas, Native American women, and Latinas. Quality control personnel (the ones we really hated) were all white women who had been upgraded from the seamstress pool, the middle managers were white women, and the top managers were all white men. Nursing homes today are similarly organized, with race and ethnic correlations for food service, janitors, licensed practical nurses (LPNs), registered nurses (RNs), case workers, and nurse managers. In general, the higher up you go, the lighter it gets, but various ethnic and racial groups have secured a toehold in specific job categories.

This organization has its roots in the *encomienda* system of planters, overseers, cane cutters, farm laborers, domestic laborers, and so on that structured both slave, conscripted, and "free" labor systems throughout the Americas (Mariátegui 2011; Vallejo 1989). During the building of the Panama Canal, even the form of payment workers received was organized by race: black workers from the West Indies were paid in silver, white workers were paid in gold. Sociologists and labor studies scholars may debate the present trends and the likely future transformations for racial organizations of the workplace, but what is striking is that this long history of racially configured labor markets has barely penetrated either classical or neoclassical economics or Marxist formulations of capitalist societies. The creative twentieth-century analyses of shifting labor market dynamics by brilliant figures such as Paul Baran and Paul Sweezy barely attended to race, and Marxists from the New Left continued the tradition. Even Thomas Piketty's new and improved theory barely mentions race and gender (see Eisenstein 2014). There is yet to be a fully articulated theory of capitalism that offers an integrated analysis.

Within whiteness studies, class differences, however, are seldom ignored. The increasingly dramatic class divide we see charted for us in the daily business reports shows reduced wages for whiteness, and even the white poor are denied a safety net of any kind. As the wages of whiteness fall, it may be tempting to see the major social divide as one of class, to argue that if white workers would simply vote like workers, we could have an effective progressive movement. It is their whiteness – that is, their *belief* that whiteness matters – that gets in the way of such a generic social movement.

The counter argument I would make is simply that a political discourse not grounded in reality cannot be successful. The real world of union organizing and contract negotiations requires complex bargaining to create solidarity given the varied needs and interests of the different groups of workers (Alcoff 2007). Skilled white workers across gender differences can advance their own strength by making common cause with other sectors within the workforce, but this requires accommodation (and a critique of craft unionism in which more professionalized sectors of workers, more often white, organize themselves separately). Work rules on the job can allow language discrimination, disempower immigrants, effectively keep the skilled trades white, or exacerbate divisive hierarchies if racial, national, religious, and gendered forms of identity are ignored. Our best labor leaders and analysts recognize these facts (Smith 2007; Hartigan 1999; Fletcher and Gapasin 2008).

If we cannot formulate the interests of workers by abstractions, then we cannot replace race with class. To seek out the minimum conditions or a lowest common denominator across widely variant sectors of the racialized labor markets will always endanger a fallback position that focuses on predictable subsets of workers. Racial progress cannot happen in the absence of an analysis of class structures and ideologies, but the same is true of progress for workers: no gains are possible with regard to the exploitation of labor without addressing race. As more and more white workers find themselves in an unprotected economic free fall, these are critical lessons to be learned in order to improve their own situation.

The Problem of the One and the Many

A third main challenge to developing a theoretical focus on whiteness is the problem of diversity within the category. This is the same challenge faced by any account of identity: the ancient problem of the one and the many (Spelman 1988). White identities are not one kind of thing, but many kinds of things, given the ways that whiteness is always mediated by other factors such as class, geographical region, age, religion, citizenship, gender, ethnicity, able-bodiedness, sexuality, language, as well as quite specifically individual variables involving a person's particular kind of schooling and family environment. The complex constellation of white identities that results resists any unified description in regard to racism, racial consciousness, or political orientation. The question, then, is whether there is any legitimacy in our talk of a "one."

Because of these mediations of identity, some white people have experienced discrimination and stereotyping that are analogous to the racism experienced by nonwhites, while other white identities have had little to no such experiences. Some can draw on experiences of homophobia, anti-Italian or anti-Polish stereotyping, or anti-rural prejudices, any of which could conceivably hold useful lessons about the harms of racism. Most whites work in fairly modest jobs, as do most people of color. Some whites are urban hipsters with trust funds, but plenty of others work at Walmart. Do these various differences suggest that the category of whiteness has decreasing explanatory utility, or none at all?

The importance of the ethnic differences among whites in the United States varies by region and sometimes even by neighborhood. In my experience, ethnicity is more important among whites in the north than it is in the south. The idea that whiteness was invisible to whites themselves – a widespread claim among the early sociologists of whiteness – never made sense to me from the perspective of growing up in the south (see, e.g., Frankenberg 1993). In this sense, the subjective life of whiteness varies as a factor of context. Under Jim Crow, whiteness was no less visible for the fact that it did not require the practices of marking or announcing used with nonwhites (as lampooned by the title "National Black Correspondent" on Jon Stewart's *Daily Show*) because whiteness was the *normative* identity – normative for "Americans," for professionals, for leaders in all fields. Whiteness went unnamed because white presence required no explanation or justification, not because it was invisible. Whiteness was always a critical element of social situations, determining the possibilities for action and modes of interaction. The commonly used phrase, "That's mighty white of you," that one can find in movies as soon as talkies began, as well as in novels like Sinclair Lewis's *Babbitt*, reveals this awareness.[1] When Katherine Hepburn declares in the 1938 film *Bringing Up Baby*, "I am free, white, and over 21," she is saying she has three positive goods that enable her to do what she wants. One cannot navigate a segregated or hierarchical social landscape without becoming schooled in the specific practices accorded to one's identity, wherever one stands with respect to the divide.

Whiteness still carries some predictive capacity in standardized test performances, treatments by police, wealth, home ownership and real estate values. Whiteness tracks electoral preferences at the national level when combined with age, gender, and having an urban or rural zip code. The likelihood of unemployment still tracks race, as does the length of incarceration upon conviction, or being chosen for the school "gifted and talented program." Although we need more studies that disaggregate racial groups, racial identity still works as a predictor for a host of significant social phenomena (Wise 2009, 2012).

The historic 2008 presidential election of Barack Obama altered our understanding of how whiteness operates as a predictor of voting patterns, since it lost some of its stand-alone predictive ability. Whiteness by itself was not a useful predictor of whether a voter would support Obama: 43

---

1 Lewis, of course, was making use of the phrase for social criticism. See Lewis 1922.

percent of whites voted for him, but this percentage was basically the same as that of whites who voted for the last two Democratic presidents, Carter and Clinton (who, respectively, won 47 percent and 43 percent of the white vote). It is sometimes true that racial correlations are sought when other factors might be more predictive, such as economic success, union membership, or by checking the voter's opinions on various public policies, for example. The fact that we still reach for race as a stand-alone predictor is based, no doubt, on the "historical gravity" of these identity categories, even as they morph into the present. But the fact that whiteness must today be combined with other correlations to produce reliable predictions indicates that it has not lost its relevance altogether (Frankenberg 1997).

The problem of the one and the many not only concerns the variations within white communities, but also the variations among nonwhite groups, along with the muddy and moveable boundaries of whiteness. Economist William A. "Sandy" Darity has overseen numerous studies that show surprisingly negligible differences between whites and light-skinned blacks in terms of job success, indicating the significant changes of the post-civil rights era (see, e.g., Darity et al. 1996). And yet, what Darity's work also shows is that, when those light-skinned black folks are disaggregated from the overall statistics on black unemployment, black poverty, and so on, the gap is even larger than we might have thought. The majority of African Americans, in other words, are even worse off vis-à-vis the majority of whites than overly generalized statistics can reveal. Darity's work shows that, while whiteness may not be necessary for job success, *lightness* still is, indicating a color hierarchy that extends beyond whites themselves.

The larger theoretical and methodological point we might conclude from these considerations of the complexity of whiteness is that the one, so to speak, will be found through a careful attentiveness to the many. Attending to the variability within categories may cause us to redefine their borders and give more weight to certain mediating factors. For rural, non-union, white men, their whiteness may well loom larger in their identity configuration than it does for other whites. Thus do identities shift and transform.

It remains critical to acknowledge that whiteness remains importantly distinct from the experiences of light-skinned or culturally assimilated nonwhites. The lived experience of white privilege connects to a unique set of historical experiences and an ongoing cultural imaginary that affects subject-formation differently for white people than it does for others, as the trove of recently published, rich phenomenologies and reflexive autobiographies is beginning to reveal (e.g. Cuomo and Hall 1999; Sullivan 2005; MacMullan 2009; Senna 1998a, 1998b, 2011). Guilt over slavery and colonialism differentiates whites from others, and whites are positioned differently within both nationalist narratives and global ones regarding "civilization," affecting both perception and self-perception. Whiteness and lightness are not identical in the conceptual imaginary that informs these narratives about who is at the vanguard of the nation, or of the species. The problem of the one and the many should remind us of the variability and fluidity intrinsic to these large categories so that we deploy them with more care and rigor. It does not yet establish their disutility.

I have so far argued that categories of social identity are sometimes organic manifestations of historical processes that create subjects, form concepts, explain social dynamics, and track patterns of perceptual judgment. This provides a general orientation to the way in which we might think about what identities are and how they arise. I have also argued that the problem of the "many" does not incapacitate our ability to speak of the "one." Let me turn now to this "one" in regard to whiteness itself.

What Do We Mean When We Talk About "Whiteness?"

Projects of inquiry that offer what seem to be conflicting accounts are sometimes simply talking about different things, or different aspects of the same thing. I will argue that, when we talk about identities of any sort, we may be talking about three related but distinct kinds of things: an empirically measurable social kind, an imaginary or representational kind, or a process for the formation of particular kinds of selves. We can regard these as three distinctive aspects of a social identity: (1) its empirical status, or the ways in which an identity can be objectively located, measured, and traced out historically in time and space; (2) its imaginary status, or the ways in which it constitutes a shared social imaginary that organizes and prescribes normative or acceptable lifestyles, both for the in-group as well as for outsiders; and (3) its subject-formation, or the constitution of individual subjects with particular ways of experiencing and perceiving as well as interacting with the social and natural environment. All three of these elements, to be adumbrated below, should be taken into account before we assess whether the "theory" of whiteness as a category serves an explanatory function, as well as what, precisely, it helps to explain.

In regard to whiteness, I will refer to these via shorthand as (1) empirical whiteness, (2) imaginary whiteness, and (3) subjective whiteness. At the beginning of this chapter I developed a four-part account of the grounds for thinking that a social identity is in fact real, involving explanatory capacity, materiality, relevance to subjectivity, and being an effect of history. The purpose of that schema was to show that the realism of identity claims is not simply about ideological effects but about the way the social world works to produce identities that can then be referred to as real. The three-part schema I will elaborate below has a different purpose: to separate out the three major aspects of whiteness.[1] In this way we can avoid talking past one another when we talk about whiteness. I also hope this approach will help signal the transformative capacity of the category of whiteness, and its multiply mediated forms.

It will be helpful to distinguish these three aspects, although the very next question will be: how are they related, causally or otherwise? Does empirical whiteness cause imaginary whiteness and the process of white subject-formation? Or vice versa? I will return to this question at the end of the chapter.

Social identities are not mainly forms of self-ascription that require a conscious investment before they can be operationalized. If this were so, then a social identity such as whiteness would be dependent upon how it is articulated and understood by the person who is said to have the identity. Yet social identities have an effect in a manner well beyond individual control, even independent of self-ascription, because they have an effect on our immediate social and familial context and how we are treated by others throughout our lives.

Structuralists may be concerned that my talk of the imaginary and of subjectivity is excessive, since so much about social identities has to do with the economic opportunities we are born into. Yet, as Du Bois instructed us, to talk about white identities in any full and meaningful sense requires that we go beyond the structural correlations of power and resources that accrue differentially across groups to consider as well the subtle and deep ways that individuals are formed. We need, then, to consider these three distinct aspects of what it means to talk about "whiteness."

---

1 I also like David Owen's tripartite division of whiteness as involving social identity, cultural representation, and assets or properties (Owen 2007a). My account clearly overlaps with his, but also differs: the concept of the imaginary as I use it is not simply about representation, but about what fuels identity formation, and the concept of the empirical is meant to be much broader than assets and property.

Empirical Whiteness

Whiteness can be studied empirically as an objective entity, with an approximate date of emergence, a set of ethnic correlations, a history, and various economic and political correlations. Recent scholarship, some in interdisciplinary whiteness studies and some in traditional disciplines, is revealing a wealth of such empirical facts, despite the usual academic disagreements and debates over methodology.

This scholarship has revealed, for example, that whiteness has a definite history, as already discussed (Painter 2012; Roediger 1991, 1994, 1998; Guglielmo 2003; Domínguez 1997). Whiteness as a consciously articulated category of identity emerged in the modern period, included only certain European ethnic groups, and was linked to an overt ideology of racial biologism, cultural vanguardism, and the legitimation narratives of colonial conquest. Some historical studies follow whiteness in general, while others consider the history of specific groups in relation to white identity, such as Italians or the Irish who were slow to "become white," or the complicated cases of Jewish identity or Latino identity, both of which have had an unstable relationship to whiteness. Besides historical work, there is also an economics of whiteness that measures persistent differentials of income and assets to quantify the effects of white skin privilege. Wealth is a much more significant indicator than wages, given that wealth accumulates through a family's history and through home ownership, thus magnifying white advantage across the generations.

Much of the empirical work on whiteness has recently emerged because social scientists from a variety of disciplines no longer define their object of study in unmarked or undifferentiated ways. Most scholars in sociology, political science, geography, women's studies, and other disciplines now routinely check to see whether their studies are specific to certain groups or are truly generalizable (Ladner

1973). As "whiteness" has lost its unmarked, default status, we now have more scholarship on white women in the military, or white men's level of participation in sports, or white family formation.

One result of this is that it is now possible to put together what might be called a geography of whiteness, a spatial terrain subject to mapping that can tell us where most whites tend to live (in integrated but not white-minority neighborhoods), where they send their kids to schools (ditto), and where they retire (Arizona: no surprise). This white or white-dominant space can then be analyzed in relation to poverty, education, real estate values, political participation, and other factors. There is a sociology of whiteness that studies patterns of reproduction, adoption, marriage, and cross-generational interaction, as well as particular practices of consumption, religious observance, leisure activities, attitudes toward health professionals and toward the police. And there is a political science of whiteness that establishes the statistical correlations between white identity and voting patterns, as well as views about political policy issues not all of which are centrally about race. Protagonists in the electoral arena are particularly interested in these dynamics, using them at times to craft "dog-whistle" discursive methods that make thinly veiled appeals to what they think are typical of whites' point of view.

To repeat the point made earlier, we should remain wary of overgeneralizations in any empirical work on whiteness or any other identity category; we need to critically reflect on whether the chosen category of analysis is really the best way to cut the grain for explanatory or predictive results. Correlations do not by themselves establish causation and can obscure as much as they reveal, and foregrounding intergroup differences can obscure significant intragroup difference. This is a reminder to take identities as small theories, subject to ongoing tests for adequacy and explanatory utility. But much of the spate of new empirical work on whiteness is on the whole descriptive, rather than explanatory. In other words, it is not offering whiteness as a sufficient cause of the phenomenon measured.

Despite these needed warnings, the recent empirical scholarship on whiteness is producing a rich trove of information on the history, the economics, the geography, the sociology, and the politics of white identity. Without a doubt, "whiteness" as a category has an empirical referent. But the imaginary representation of whiteness is just as important to study.

Imaginary Whiteness

By this, I mean to refer to the realm of mythic imagery and the relatively unconscious ways in which people have affective and dispositional attitudes about whiteness – that is, what whiteness stands for, what it means, its imagined genealogy, and how it is qualitatively distinct from other groups. In psychoanalysis, the concept of the imaginary has a very specific meaning within a theory of ego-formation, involving a process of self-alienation as the subject tries to construct an imaginary self that is whole, coherent, and independent. Freudian theorists of identity tend to conclude from this that the process of forming a self-identity is necessarily problematic to the extent it seeks to construct a kind of false image by deemphasizing the fragmented and fluid nature of human experience. I am skeptical, as I have argued elsewhere (Alcoff 2006), that such an account of subject-formation is truly universalizable across every historical context of identity formations. Thus, my use of the term "imaginary" should not signify allegiance to the Freudian tradition.

Although the white imaginary is no doubt motivated at least in part by the desire to construct a livable self, as Freud hypothesized, I want to use the concept in a less technical sense. I prefer the way that feminist philosophers Michele LeDoeuff (1990) and Moira Gatens (1995) have used the imaginary to denote a collective rather than individual background layer of understandings and dispositions that both enables and constrains our ability to produce new ideas and responses. In this sense, the concept "imaginary" signals something that is not so much based on actual historical experiences as on a shared orientation that may be quite at odds with any accurate version of real events. Consider as an example the imaginary that is prompted by the US flag. To understand the meanings and effects of the stars and stripes, it will never be sufficient merely to detail its history or its current institutional uses; we need also to consider the visual and ideational connotations and affective elements that the flag engenders for diverse groups and individuals. When we see the flag, do we imagine George Washington, or Fort Sumter (the site of the start of the US Civil War), soldiers in World War II or in Iraq, or the flag that flies over various colonial sites, from Guam to Panama to the Virgin Islands?

It would be a mistake to think that the sphere of the imaginary is completely distinct from the sphere of rational action. In fact, the imaginary of whiteness can drive the articulation of our rational interests, given our attachment to a certain self-understanding and what is required for social respect or acknowledgment. Whites have demonstrably chosen race-based over economic interests when, for example, they choose to work for less pay in a non-union hospital with a larger white workforce rather than in a unionized hospital with a diverse workforce, or when they vote for white candidates less likely to deliver services they need than for candidates associated with multiracial constituencies. Or just when they stop watching their favorite sports, whether it is baseball or basketball, because of the predominance of nonwhite players (even golf is now in jeopardy!).

As the economists George Akerlof and Rachel Kranton (2010) show, traditional and decontextualized notions of rational utility-maximizing self-interests, whether for monetary gain or personal pleasure, cannot explain the preferential patterns we continue to witness. Akerlof and Kranton develop the concept of "identity utility" to explain prefer-ences that make sense in the context of group-related norms but that look inexplicable – or simply irrational – outside this frame. A preference may have no economic value and yet have identity value. I am suggesting that the concept of the white imaginary can help us to understand these norms of behavior and assessments of our self-inter-est. It is the white imaginary that constructs our "identity utility," such as the desire to be in white dominant spaces. Such desires and needs then become part of a person's rational self-interest. We might attempt to charitably con-strue such preferences as being simply driven by a univer-sal experience of having a higher comfort level with people of our "own kind." But the white imaginary is determining who we can imagine our "own kind" to be.

As Alain Locke astutely observed in 1925:

> For generations the Negro has been the peasant matrix of
> that section of America which has most undervalued him,
> and here he has contributed not only materially in labor
> and in social patience, but spiritually as well...the fact [is]
> that a leaven of humor, sentiment, imagination and tropic
> nonchalance has gone into the making of the South from
> a humble, unacknowledged source. (1997/1925, 15)

Even when there is no blood relation of a biological sort, there is a kinship of culture and experience born of centu-ries of syncretism and cultural amalgamations inevitable to sharing a land and generally living in close proximity.

The black bluegrass musical group, the Carolina Choco-late Drops, has bravely, brilliantly, and with great heart explored this syncretic history in their retrieval of two centuries of traditional folk tunes, including those from the period of the minstrels along with the Sea Islands, the Delta blues, and the Scottish Gaelic-singing settlers of South Carolina. They demonstrate the borrowing of instru-ments, rhythms, cadence, and lyrical content, constructing utopian moments of folk music collaborations out of a historical context of dystopian realities. The band insists that this reminder of the South's syncretism is not about redemption, and they never let their audiences forget the cruel terms by which cultural differences were forcibly fused. But revealing the actual syncretisms that emerged in such spaces advances our self-understanding. We need to come to an understanding of the multiple sources of what we think of as "southern," or "American."

Such efforts can help us assess more perceptively and more critically how the white imaginary, or the imaginary of whiteness, is being produced, and how xenophobia is manufactured through a falsification of reality. Imaginary whiteness is particularly illustrative of Louis Althusser's (1971) definition of ideology as an imaginary relationship to the real. And, like other ideologies, imaginary whiteness has very real and material effects.

On the one hand, if one feels this strongly about one's connection to white people and to a white dominant community or nation, then it is rational in some sense to make choices that manifest this preference. But, on the other hand, truly rational behavior should not simply pursue one's preferences but should consider how those preferences are produced and whether they conflict with one's other needs and commitments. The concept of imaginary whiteness can thus help to foreground not the empirical or material realities of whiteness, but the falsified grounds for white preferences, self-conceptions, and identifications.

It is not necessarily the case that every form of social identity is equally based on the sorts of "false origin" stories that theorist Max Weber argued was the foundation of ethnicity. Not every "imaginary" related to social identity is equally deceptive. But the white imaginary can also influence people who are not white.

The importance of addressing whiteness at the level of the imaginary is critical because it affects our ability to imagine a different future. The recent work in whiteness studies, however theoretically sophisticated, also provides a text for reading the cultural unconscious (mostly of whites) about what whiteness has been and can become (see e.g. Yancy 2005). Even while this scholarship has helpfully showcased the heterogeneity within and among white people, it has also tended to tie the very idea of whiteness irrevocably to racism. This can make it rather difficult to engender a different imaginary in which whiteness becomes part of a diverse coalition for social change and social justice.

Whiteness figures in a distinct and unique way in the imaginary rendering of the history of the United States and of the West more generally. There are both falsehoods and truths that contribute to the mythic representations in this historical narrative. For example, it is notably false to say that Columbus *discovered* America because, let's be honest, he stumbled on it by mistake, and continued to believe until his death that his ships had reached some part of Asia. What actually occurred was less a discovery than an encounter between several cultures followed rather quickly by invasion, genocide, enslavement, and the annexation of lands. By continuing to use the term "discovery," such unpleasant facts are downplayed in the typical Columbus Day celebrations of exploratory adventurism, and agency is conferred on only one side of the confrontation. There are many other such falsehoods and half-truths still contributing to the currents of the white imaginary – concerning the genesis of science, literature, poetics, mathematics, philosophy, democracy, bicameral legislatures, and the existence of cannibalism. This last idea – that the indigenous were cannibals – was actually based on a third-hand rumor that ship-hands taken in 1493 by the Carib Indians were never seen again. (Would you willingly leave a Caribbean island to work in servitude below deck aboard a primitive, overcrowded schooner?)

But if the imaginary domain of whiteness is made up of these falsehoods and half-truths, there are also *truths* about white identity, such as a voluntary (relatively speaking) migration, widespread participation in land annexation and racist terror, and, importantly, centuries of being the psychic beneficiary of representations as the hard-working heart of America. Civil rights for African Americans was not won until African Americans collectively organized, and it is doubtful that the equal rights of undocumented workers will be won until they can somehow force the hand of the state. Whites as a group cannot take much if any credit for these movements to make the Constitution more than a hypocritical document riven by contradictions, and, to this extent, the history of white recalcitrance on social equality is glaring.

Imaginary whiteness is not simply the repository of unreason: some versions of it, at least, can be linked to real historical experiences that congeal into images informing the interpretation and judgment of new events. In fact, the acknowledgment of racist injustice also informs many whites' own imaginary about white identity, I would suggest. This aspect of the white imaginary can explain the patterns of behavior – denial, avoidance, self-segregation – we might think of as resulting from a guilty conscience.

Projections of inferiority on the groups unjustly treated by whites then serves the helpful purpose of explaining away racist violence, softening the sense of guilt, and legitimating the legacies of unequal distributions that whites enjoy today. The persistent attachment to a racism increasingly disconfirmable by easily available evidence, then, might be explained precisely by this guilty conscience, this acknowledgment of past wrong. Paradoxically, this may give us some cause for hope.

Subjective Whiteness

The third aspect of whiteness that merits analysis is the relationship between whiteness and the self. The idea that there is a specifically *white* way of being in the world, initially inspired by the work of W.E.B. Du Bois and Frantz Fanon, has been more recently explored in the work of philosophers Charles Mills, Shannon Sullivan, Terrance

MacMullan, and David Owen, as well as by an increasing number of sociologists, anthropologists, and cultural analysts. The upshot of this work is to bring the substantive specificity of white subjective experience into relief. Whiteness is not in fact a racially unmarked human experience, despite the fact that whiteness has been taken as the default position of the human. Hence, white subjectivity is not so different from other racialized groups.

Whites do tend to have, however, their own peculiar inclinations, affects, practices, and modes of perception. Mills has developed the influential idea that whites operate with what he calls an epistemology of ignorance: a set of substantive epistemic practices designed to protect their belief that society is basically a meritocracy, people of color are responsible for their troubles, and racism is a thing of the past. Mills's persuasive point is that, in our shared world, with its recurrent headlines about police shootings and disparities in poverty and unemployment, it takes no small amount of *work* to interpret these facts as consistent with raceless meritocracies. "Part of what it means to be constructed as white," he reasons, is to operate with "a cognitive model that precludes self-transparency and genuine understanding of social realities" (1997, 18). This means that white children are systematically taught to become delusional.

Sullivan (2005, 2014) and MacMullan (2009) have each offered more phenomenological descriptions of what it is like to live on the inside of white identities developed in white supremacist societies. Sullivan explores in great detail what she calls the unconscious and seductive habits of white privilege that organize our patterns of social interaction. By calling these "habits," Sullivan seeks to turn our attention to bodily practices below the level of conscious intent that involve forms of attentiveness, assumptions of entitlement to space and to freedom of movement, and a routine disregard for nonwhite others. She draws from the psychoanalytic theories of Jean LaPlanche to explain how these habitual dispositions are passed down through the generations, not through consciously articulated claims (at least, not all the time) but through more subtle bodily signs of aversion and distrust. She concludes from this that present day whites are mistaken in thinking they have nothing at all in common with previous generations in their families who were more overtly racist. MacMullan uses the phrase "vessel of racist habits" with a similar intent to get at the ways in which people are inculcated into certain behaviors and attitudes before they are aware of what is happening. More than Sullivan, MacMullan argues that this way of being in the world is ultimately against white interests: in fact, he holds that whites have more to gain than lose in facing the reality of racist oppression. The white world as currently constructed offers numbness or disaffection, a sense of emptiness and cultural vacuity, and unassuaged guilt. But MacMullan and Sullivan share the view that these problematic and dysfunctional aspects of white subjectivity are not irremediable. Rendering our habits visible makes them accessible for reflection and evaluation. This is a possible route for change.

To say, then, that whiteness is involved in the constitution of the self means that our core set of routine perceptual and epistemic practices and our everyday habits of social interaction, interpretation, and judgment need to be analyzed in relation to a specific racialization process involving whiteness. Such phenomena are not universal: other groups may have less of an investment in epistemologies of ignorance and their very survival may require better epistemic habits, such as the need to listen carefully to what others have to say. We need to recognize that whiteness is not simply about our conscious awareness, nor is it simply about structural patterns of social inequality or cultural representations that we can simply repudiate. We also need to avoid assuming that everyone undergoes an essentially generic and universal process of personality formation that is only afterward connected to racialized differences. In sum, just as an earlier generation of feminists insisted that gender patterns were distorting the normative frame of "personality tests," so we need to bring race into our account of the formation of subjectivity.

Although white subjectivity can have distinct elements, this work still raises a question about the racialization of other kinds of subjects. If whiteness is constitutive of the self, is *latinidad*? Or blackness? Or indigeneity? We should not jump to analogies that might universalize a process of subject-formation involving relational superiority and sharp differentiation, or an unreflective manner in which habits of perception and judgment develop. Whiteness (like maleness in this regard, and other normative identity categories) has been defined as having a selfhood distinct from others – smarter, more culturally advanced, more typically rational, and thus naturally on top of the social pyramid. No other group has enjoyed this position within mass, high, *and* popular culture. When this vanguard position is threatened, we see whites lash out in ways that make it appear their very sense of self is at stake: merely implying that their lineage might be "polluted" by "one drop" is sometimes denied beyond all reason. The philosopher/artist Adrian Piper (1992–3) suggested the following as a test of antiracism: not whether one, as a white person, could commit oneself to ending racism, but whether one could imagine oneself as *being* black. Whiteness does not appear to be *experienced* as a peripheral or contingent characteristic, but as a feature of what the Greeks called *haeceity* or thisness, meaning that without which the thing no longer is what it is. Far from being invisible to whites themselves, whiteness appears to be the cornerstone of their sense of who they are. Hybridity is not as much as a threat to other racial identities, nor are there assumptions of global, comparative superiority in every group. All forms of subjectivity may not be equally vulnerable to the threatened loss of cultural dominance.

There are two senses, then, in which we might think of whiteness as constitutive of the self: (a) because whiteness plays a role in constituting relatively unconscious habits and practices, and (b) because whiteness is *consciously* experienced as an essential property to the self. These work independently, meaning that even individuals who do not consciously experience whiteness as central to their self may still be profoundly affected by the unconscious habits and practices commonly associated with white identity.

Besides the philosophical accounts of white subject-formation, which rely mostly on phenomenology and history, there is a burgeoning body of empirical research different in kind from that discussed in the category I named "empirical whiteness," since, rather than objectively measuring racial inequities or unearthing the political history of the concept, this research reveals the subjective dimensions of whiteness. The field of social psychology is the main player. Claude Steele (2010), former Director of the Center for Behavioral Sciences at Stanford, developed numerous experiments to reveal unconscious dispositions with respect to racial difference that affect test performance, confidence, social interaction, and conversational approaches. As it turns out, racialized "priming" can increase whites' confidence and performance, while simultaneously decreasing that of others, when the idea is conveyed before a test that whites tend to perform better. Steele's suggestion is that our everyday cultural environment provides such priming on a regular basis through the communication of identity stereotypes; no manipulating psychology experimenters need to be around. The priming phenomenon affects everybody's confidence and performance; the only difference is that, for whites and males, prevailing identity stereotypes almost always help rather than hurt.

Steele's research has documented the unconscious modes of interaction posited by philosophers such as Mills and Sullivan. In his most famous experiment, two white male subjects (usually Stanford undergraduates) are told that they are going to participate in a conversation on the topic of either love or race, with a third person who has not yet arrived. The psychologist then casually flips to a chart that reveals a picture of the third conversation partner; in some cases, the two white subjects can see that they will be conversing with a black man, in other cases with a white man. At that point the psychologist says he or she has to step out for a moment, and asks the two white male subjects if they wouldn't mind arranging the chairs in the room for the conversation. You can guess what happens next – the chair arranging is recorded through a two-way mirror and, with an alarmingly high rate of predictability, white males will arrange the chairs much closer together when they know that the third conversant is going to be white, or when the topic of the conversation is going to be love. When the third conversant is going to be black and the topic of conversation is going to be race, the chairs are set as far apart as the room will allow.

There are loads of such experiments that support the idea that our unconscious attitudes about other groups affect how we interact, whether we lean forward in conversation or turn slightly away, whether we maintain eye contact, are expressive, smile, or are awkward and stumble over our words. (Gladwell 2005, 85–6). In another experiment, white anxiety about cross-racial encounters is tested in the following way (Richeson and Trawalter 2008). White subjects are asked to interact with a person they have never met, who is, in some cases, as in the chair-arranging experiment, white and in other cases black. After the interaction, the subjects are given simple cognitive tests designed to reveal their mental acuity. The results are clear: the whites who had had to interact with a black person made numerous simple mistakes in comparison to the control group. They were mentally fatigued. The demands of interracial interaction even of this innocuous sort diminished their cognitive skills. There is more than one way to explain this result – the fatigue may be due to extreme discomfort caused by racism or it might be due to heightened vigilance motivated by an anxiety that they will appear racist (or actually make a racist comment). But any of these explanations would indicate that the existence of racial difference affects how whites interact in ways that cannot be easily controlled.

If these effects are not understood to be features of white subjectivity, they may be blamed on the nonwhite people who trigger discomfort, unease, etc. But the research shows that the personality of the nonwhite person is irrelevant to the results. From this burgeoning research, we can conclude that whiteness impacts perceptual attunements and modes of interaction as well as the associations and connotations that affect judgment. How can we then not conclude that whiteness is constitutive of the self?

The empirical, imaginary, and subjective aspects of white identity are not entirely separate or separable. The white imaginary surely affects, or infects, subject-formation, which in turn affects the social interaction and judgments that produce some of the empirical social realities of race. But this way of formulating the relation is overly idealist; the material context of our lives surely impacts our judgment, modes of interaction, and assumptions about others. Stupid ideas hang on because they resonate in some way with our material realities. We (women and men alike) sometimes believe women are naturally vain creatures who prefer to spend a great deal of their time on their physical appearance because that is what we see most women doing; we (whites and nonwhites alike) sometimes believe whites are smarter because we see them dominating the most intellectually demanding jobs.

A better understanding of the relationship between the empirical, the imaginary, and the subjective whiteness is that they form a mutually supporting holistic set, rather than a linear line of causation with any one aspect as the determining condition. The circle can be broken, dislodged, challenged, fragmented, and so on, at multiple entry points, such as the policies of affirmative action that enforce changes in our lived material work space, rectifying vanguard narratives in educational curricula and popular culture. Even the efforts to reveal implicit biases and tacit knowledge embedded in forms of subjectivity can produce a reflexive moment of self-alteration.

Yet, describing these three aspects of whiteness as they currently exist – the empirical, the imaginary, and the way in which whiteness is constitutive of the self – cannot help but foreground racism as a constitutive feature of our realities, making it truly seem as if whiteness is irretrievably tied to racism. Is it?

− 2 −

White Exceptionalism

He could now see his life opening before him, uncomplex and inescapable as a barren corridor, completely freed now of ever again having to think or decide, the burden which he now assumed and carried as bright and weightless and martial as his insignatory brass: a sublime and implicit faith in physical courage and blind obedience, and a belief that the white race is superior to any and all other races and that the American is superior to all other white races and that the American uniform is superior to all men, and that all that would ever be required of him in payment for this belief, this privilege, would be his own life.

William Faulkner, *Light in August*, 1932

William Faulkner, raised in Mississippi at the beginning of the twentieth century, wrote a set of severe novels exposing the perverted logic of white supremacy and the high price extracted from everyone who succumbed to its claims, including whites. However, Faulkner not only critically exposed the illogic of white racism, he also exemplified it. He castigated segregation as "obsolete and unjust" yet boasted that he would go armed to the streets to meet federal troops sent to Mississippi to dismantle it. In this chapter, I want to consider the pessimism and fatalism about white racism that might engender this contradictory attitude, the sort of attitude many have about so many atrocious social phenomena today: "it's terrible, but it will never change." I hold Faulkner's fatalism to be more emblematic of his failures as an artist, and as a man, than of his astute capacities for social criticism.

Faulkner's work is too often mistakenly treated as symptomatically southern. In truth, his probing diagnostics simply zeroed in on the *rural* form in which our home-grown version of Plato's Myth of the Metals took shape throughout the United States, classifying human kinds by a ranking system based on visible phenotype. Faulkner obsessively returned over and over to the points when phenotype failed to deliver, when the visible misled, a situation he portrayed as the inevitable prelude to tragedy. The passage cited at the start of this chapter is a silent rumination of a mixed race man named Joe Christmas who was passing for white. Christmas cruelly murders the white woman who loved him for fear she would expose his secret. When his crime, along with his African lineage, is discovered by the local townspeople, a lynching is inevitable. Faulkner's humanism was manifest in his compassion for such complex victims, despite his dogged pessimism about the original sin of race. But pessimism breeds the fatalism that excuses inaction and complicity.

In this chapter, I want to consider the bounds of our collective pessimism about racism, and, in particular, about white racism. A pessimism worthy of Faulkner, but too little examined, drives the idea of what I call "white exceptionalism": the idea that whiteness is so distinct as a form of social identity and so problematically tied to its supremacist illusions that it cannot be redeemed.

Faulkner had a tragic sensibility about racism, so much so that he was incapable of imagining a world where it might have a little less bite. His literature rendered the social world of segregation and the quest for racial purity profound, mysterious, and intractable. Despite the fact that he knew the lie of purity and willingly explored the elements of syncretism in southern white society, he failed to see racisms' flexibility and instability. Other white writers of the time, such as Flannery O'Connor or Howard Fast, similarly focused on segregated societies but offered more complicated pictures.

However, Faulkner's contradictory impulses mirrored common white racist sensibilities of the era, in which segregationists routinely avowed their concern and affection for black people. Historian Jason Sokol's fascinating portrait of white southern attitudes toward civil rights, appropriately titled *There Goes My Everything* (2006), documents these avowals in newspaper reports, personal narratives, and interviews from the time. "Most of us have a deep and abiding affection for the Negro," one typical Mississippi native recounts (2006, 57). Violence was only necessary, such men believed, when the rules of nature were abrogated. As long as segregation was upheld, everyday interactions could be enacted on the model of a kind paternalism, or so whites thought. A more perceptive analysis given by a white South Carolinian, from the hindsight of the late 1960s, noted the utility of these contradictions: "In our inmost [ears], we knew we were wrong, and so...we didn't talk about justice, we talked about love" (Sokol 2006, 58).

Maybe affection was quite truly felt, but what was it they were feeling the affection for? Consider this. The resounding majority of white southerners expressed surprise at the movement for civil rights; middle-class whites were convinced their servants were content. The "trouble," as they called the movement, was caused by Yankees, communists, and Jews. Sokol finds in community after community white perplexity, surprise, and resistance to the idea that African Americans wanted social equality. And they compounded this error with a claim of epistemic privilege *as white southerners*, claiming to be in a privileged position to "know" black people. The owner of a lumber mill in Albany, Georgia, expressed this idea without a blush, assuring "his fellow white southerners that federal judges 'simply don't know the American Negro as you and I do'" (Sokol 2006, 69). Whites thought they knew black people, and they liked what they thought they knew. In truth, the affection such fellows might have felt was for a mask held up to soothe their egos and relax their trigger fingers.

Most of the white people in numerous parts of the world who today employ nonwhite nannies, maids, and gardeners undoubtedly have the same illusions about what their employees think about the conditions of their employment, and about their white employers. Such illusions can only be maintained by denial, avoidance, an unwillingness to investigate, or a disinterest in doing so.

Without doubt, the most particular and exceptional aspect of whiteness as compared to other social identities is its historic relationship to racism. This attachment trumps reason and logic and even, as Faulkner knew, self-interest. Historians of the idea of race unite in the view that one cannot understand its emergence except as a kind of discursive maneuver, conjuring facts that would support preferred narratives of natural hierarchy and benign social stewardship. Ivan Hannaford voices typical impatience with "the uncritical acceptance of the concept of race" and of specious "facts" about common blood and the like "enshrined as 'givens' in value-free studies of race and the course of daily life" (1996, 3–4). To read historical studies of racial ideas is to read a cohort of irritated historians.

If race is a myth, whiteness is, some argue, the driving plotline. Even the nuanced studies of Nell Painter that portray whiteness as a complex multiplicity – with periodic expansions from an initial Teutonic/Saxon/Anglo-Saxon strain – suggest that *all* the expansions in the definitions and boundaries of whiteness have been motivated by the need to differentiate white people from the African, at all costs (2010, 210). Gerald Horne (2014) dates the inception of this formulation, of whiteness as top dog, as none other than 1776, the moment when whites (or at least, white men) became enfranchised over and against indigenous

peoples and all those from the African diaspora. Revolutionary triumph against the British thus sealed the fate of
these groups, worsening their political and material futures,
including their very right to live. Hence, far from the
popular "creation myth" of the United States as a progressive minded polity striving for freedom, Horne sees the
founding of the US nation, not unreasonably, as the first
apartheid state, similar to the founding of Rhodesia.

Omi and Winant followed up their concept of racial
formations with the concept of *racial projects* as a way to
make sense of the political elements attached to racial
concepts. A racial project, on their view, is an interpretation or representation of race that is linked to and motivated by practical aims, such as a particular organization
of power or distribution of resources (1994, 56). Racial
projects are racial concepts with an agenda, in other words.
For many theorists, the racial project of whiteness has been
clear and consistent: to maintain a race-based distribution
of resources that will ensure the continuation of what is
actually an oligarchy. Whites as a whole will buy in, and
defend the status quo, if the distribution system favors
them even a little over nonwhites. Hence, whiteness as a
concept is tied to the agenda of racism. If whiteness, in all
its plural varieties, has been *constituted* by this racial
project, from the first moment of its political formation,
how can whiteness persist when the supremacist illusions
give way?

Arguably, without a racist motivation, the idea of amal-
gamating the plethora of European peoples, of including
the great unwashed, to quote Eliot, would have been
unnecessary. Without the colonial agenda to keep non-
European peoples down, it might well have been unnecessary to let the denigrated "south of Europe" – Jews,
Italians, Irish, Spaniards, Poles, and so on – into the club-
house, sharing close quarters with discomfited WASP elites,
not to mention brokering political power. If the economic
opportunities for black people, and *other* others, were not
so circumscribed, whiteness itself would not have the

explanatory capacity to account for the differentials in family trajectories, such as class mobility. Thus, what whiteness *explains* is racial oppression.

It is interesting to imagine how social identity categories might have evolved differently. If the category of "whiteness" had not come along, more specific and specifically locatable ethnic and national lineages might have remained. "European" identity itself might have been able to represent and accumulate all the diverse ethnicities that have long lived on the continent of Europe, without limitation by race, thus including the significant numbers of new ethnic formations within Europe such as Turkish Germans or French Arabs or the black Dutch. By the introduction of whiteness and other racial terms, all this organically produced fluid multiplicity was shut down and shut out. Race terms predominated to amalgamate large swaths of diversity within simplistic, and misleading, rubrics, eliding long-held antagonisms within racial groups while evading the actual syncretisms being produced amongst groups who shared close living quarters.

This history of specious gerrymandering around white identity terms is what leads David Roediger to reject the category of whiteness as "ontologically empty." Roediger may seem to be alluding to the idea that whiteness lacks substance, that it is bland and nondescript, but his claim is actually based on its history, not its thin cultural content. Whiteness, he claims, was organized not by its own substantive content, but by its differentiation from blackness, etc. The infamous "one-drop rule" (see p. 86) then begins to make a certain logical sense. If whiteness meant "not black," then only blackness, or African lineage, could alter one's social identity. Black people of mixed heritage would never qualify as white or even as partly white, as indeed, under the laws of Jim Crow and the customs of hypo-descent, they did not.

I myself would not give blackness the unique "pride of place" here to unseat white identity; other groups had this power in certain contexts. In some places indigeneity or

Mexican or Chinese identities, among others, were more serious threats. Today it is the fears about Latinos, Arabs, and Muslims that ground the nativist, xenophobic resurgence, and not primarily African Americans. If Silvio Torres-Saillant is right that blackness is always local, then surely this is also true of whiteness. Yet the point about whiteness remains: it is defined by that which it is not.

Hence Roediger concludes, following a claim Baldwin once made, that whiteness "is *nothing but* oppressive and false"(1994, 13; emphasis in original). And in this sense, whiteness is exceptional. Roediger makes no such claims about other groups demarcated by racial terms. We can speak of African American culture and community as emerging out of the conditions of slavery, or of Chicanos developing a culture from the experience of internal colonialism, to give a couple of possible examples, but on Roediger's view there is no such shared history of whiteness, no such macro event of history that formed a people from shared trauma or dislocation. For him, whiteness is defined, as the French linguist Ferdinand de Saussure might have approvingly put it, simply in terms of its difference from all that is not white. Since it has no positive or substantive content, whiteness must retain that differentiation, that borderline, that separability, or lose itself in the morass of colored gradations. And this is why whiteness itself is, Roediger claims, "a destructive ideology" (1994, 3), incapable of becoming disentangled from its racist roots, doomed to a persistent policing of borders no matter what the cost.

This idea will be the topic of the present chapter – that is, the idea that all there really is to whiteness is racism, and that without racism whiteness would not exist. If this is so, whiteness could never be included within a vision of a less racist future. I will attempt to find a position that can accommodate two truths I take to be incontrovertible: (a) that whiteness is a historical formation of racism, and its subsequent iterations have also been profoundly influenced by racist "racial projects," and (b) that racism is not all that whiteness is or has been about, and that white identities are not constitutively tied to racism for the unending future. The formation of white identity in its empirical, imaginary, and subjective elements is imbued with a racist history, albeit varied and complex, and yet whiteness is not *nothing but* racism. Let us see if these two claims can be held together in one coherent theory.

To consider whether racism is truly constitutive of whiteness, we need to understand something about the history of both the concept and the practice of whiteness. Its history may not fully determine its future permutations, so, as I offered in Chapter 1, a more complete analysis of whiteness should include an assessment of its explanatory value as well as its explanatory limitations. In the next section I will argue that in order to understand the *meaning* of whiteness we also need to understand the way *meanings* work in general as well as the way the *meaning* of white supremacy has worked in particular. White supremacy has attempted to secure a unique and exceptional place for whiteness, among the panoply of human kinds. It has attempted to fix whiteness with a unique and unalterable telos. It has portrayed whiteness as so exceptional that it cannot mix with others.

It will be helpful here to take a short tour of an old debate about color and white light that showcases two eerily familiar versions of the exceptionalist thesis.

Newton Versus Goethe

There is a famous debate between the English physicist Sir Isaac Newton and the German poet Johann Wolfgang von Goethe on the topic of the unique character of white light.[1]

---

1 Some easily available sources on this debate can be found at: http://www.thestargarden.co.uk/NewtonAndLight.html and at http://www.brainpickings.org/2012/08/17/goethe-theory-of-colours/. See also Sepper 2003. Thanks go to Ishani Maitra for initially turning me on to this debate.

The debate was only a virtual one, occurring between interlocutors who lived a century apart, but it was pointed nonetheless, and continues to spark debate among theorists of the science of color and light. The question that Newton and Goethe were each concerned to address was the following: where does white light fit within the spectrum of colored light? Where, in other words, does whiteness fit among the other colors?

Sir Isaac Newton held that whiteness has a unique character that renders it absolutely distinct. It is the only color, he argued, that includes all other colors. Through the process of diffraction, a prism refracting white light will produce the entire color spectrum, creating a rainbow effect. Since only white light has this capacity, it is unique.

Although he is known best today as a poet and dramatist of the masterwork *Faust*, Johann Wolfgang von Goethe also vigorously pursued interests in philosophy, theology, and the empirical sciences. He took a particular interest in the study of light and color. Writing about a century after Newton, Goethe took issue with the famous physicist's account about the nature of white light. Color, Goethe observed, arises in the spectrum, not from white light itself, but at the border between light and dark. Color is not subsumed *within* whiteness, as Newton thought, but emerges just at its immediate perimeter. Hence he thought we should understand white light as essentially indivisible and absolutely homogeneous, a pure entity, fundamentally separate from color.

Despite their differences, Goethe and Newton both gave white light a privileged place, not within or inside the rainbow of the color spectrum, but, as it were, over the rainbow. Moreover, their theories eerily mimic some of the most powerful ideologies of racial whiteness still prevalent today that render it a thing apart. Goethe conceives white light as a form of indivisible purity, as if a single drop of color would taint and alter its identity, and he makes this characteristic unique to whiteness. No other color is so easily besmirched by contamination. While other colors move along a continuum of shades, with gradations of intensity, only slowly changing their identity, white light, on his theory, is unique in needing to stand alone, unable to merge or survive a dilution. Against this portrayal, Newton conceived of white light as a kind of universal representation, capable of standing in for the complete color spectrum. Just as some have viewed whiteness as representing the unadulterated essence of humanity, or the true universal of the human form, so Newton viewed white light as the one universally inclusive form of light. In this sense, the entire color spectrum can be represented by whiteness, while other nonwhite colors can only represent, in a sense, their own.

One might wonder at the unconscious racial impulses that guided this famous debate, especially when we read Goethe saying, in his 1774 letter to Jacobi, that lightness "is the simplest most undivided most homogenous being that we know. Confronting it is the darkness." Goethe and Newton were both writing, after all, during the period of European colonial expansion, at a time when the types and categories of human groups were being allocated a moral and social status based on color. Whether or not either of these great theorists was exhibiting his racial unconscious, both positions helpfully illustrate, by analogy at least, alternate forms of what I am calling *white exceptionalism*.

Universalism Versus Purity

This thesis can take one of two forms. (1) One might hold, like Newton, that whiteness is more universal, and thus more representative, than any other color. It does not exist as a *part* of the rainbow, but as the *necessary condition* for the rainbow's very existence. To carry this idea forward to identity, we might surmise that, if whites are more rational, as some still believe, and if they have constituted the vanguard of science, invention, and democracy through which the species as a whole has managed to survive and continues to advance, then whiteness is indeed separate, but also representative of what is "truly" human, or of what differentiates us from the beasts, as it were. Hence, all we really need are white presidents and political leaders: their point of view is universal, able to represent everyone, while all others can only really represent "special interests." (2) One might hold, conversely, like Goethe, that white light exists in an eternal, oppositional confrontation to color. Whiteness is not so much representative of the whole as in conflict with the whole. This approach would counsel against all forms of "miscegenation" including cultural and political influences leading to syncretic or hybrid formations.

There are both racist and antiracist versions of white exceptionalism. For racists, whites are, of course, superior to other groups and in this way set apart, and set above. Racists can be white exceptionalists in either of the above two formulations, whereas antiracists can be white exceptionalists in the second formulation. Given that whiteness is distinct in the manner of its formation, accorded legal rights and protections above all others, then racial whiteness is exceptional in its intrinsic incapacity to accept equality with the "barbarians."

Hence, antiracist exceptionalists point to the fact that whiteness is qualitatively distinct in form. Of course, it is not the only social identity that has a problematic genealogy, based in hierarchy, but this does not mitigate the seriousness of the problem. If comparative superiority is central to what it means to think of oneself as white, there is no peaceful coexistence nor accommodation within the rainbow. Projects of pluralism may harmonize the differences between *other* racial groups, but the racism that constitutes white identity cannot harmonize. Leading analysts studying the structural patterns of white identity lend support to this worry (Feagin 2013; Lipsitz 1998; Hall 1995; Applebaum 2010).

Let's slow this train down a bit. What exactly does it mean when we say that the social construct of white social identity is constituted by racism? There are multiple possibilities. One might mean to say that the formative history of the concept came out of a race-based (and gender-based) colonial world order emerging from the conquest of the Americas, that it developed because it has been functional for that order, and that it would not have persisted except for this functionality. This is the kind of claim decolonial theorists such as Anibal Quijano (2008) and Walter Mignolo (2005) have been making. Making whiteness visible is often aiming to make not only its history visible but also, more importantly, its political functionality within the current oligarchy.

On this approach, the relation of whiteness to racism is historical and structural. It is not a claim about present day individual intentions, at least not yet. It is not necessarily a claim about the experiential side of white subjective identity. But it is a claim about the *meaning* of whiteness, how whiteness is grasped as a *kind*, and how it is understood as a *value*. And this is to say that, at the ideational or imaginary level, whiteness is about racism. What exactly can this mean?

Talking about ideational notions of whiteness may seem irrelevant to the actual sociological relations between groups, or, at least, not fully determinative of those relations. And the historical eras of slavery and colonialism in which white identities were first constituted have radically changed, it is true, especially in our post-civil rights era. To the extent that these notions of white superiority, such as the seventeenth-century ideas about the Great Chain of Being, still have any relevance, it is only, one might hold, in our collective unconscious as racialized subjects. In the real world, almost all of us must live, work, and function in multiracial contexts in which whiteness takes its share of hits, sometimes being the butt of the joke. Illusions of universality and purity or permanent supremacy seem to have little purchase on this quotidian reality.

And the distributive patterns of the world economy are in flux.

But it would be dangerous to underemphasize the potency of white dominance in the realm of the material and the political. Surely the imaginary of whiteness as top dog persists because of its coherence with this reality, as well as its continued functionality. The ideational aspect of whiteness, then, is not simply a historical holdover, but an ongoing player in legitimation narratives that favor the 1 percent. As Toni Morrison has described it, the white imaginary has dominated the literary imaginary in American letters, rendering our national narrative into a story about white people, even while race itself could not be thematized (Morrison 1992). If the story of the US is essentially the story of white people, then the overall story, until recently, can be played as a story of general progress. The Tea Party activists who claim that "their" America has been stolen assume that the protagonist role in this story is rightly theirs because America is *uniquely* based in "white values" and "white history," such that our imminent racial pluralism will be a game changer, bringing down the United States in a way no foreign power has even tried, much less succeeded.

American exceptionalism is the idea that the class divisions and plutocratic dangers that beset "old Europe" and emerging democracies are not relevant in the United States because of its post-ethnic melting pot, but this, in my view, is simply a deraced version of white exceptionalism. In other words, American exceptionalism is white exceptionalism posing, or passing, as a nonracial theory. The entire hemisphere of the Americas has been a melting pot of race and ethnicity for 500 years, and in the last 200 years this has developed in the context of troubled but vibrant democratic cultures, but this is somehow ignored. Faulkner had his character's ruminations seamlessly move from race to nation, from intergroup supremacy to intragroup supremacy, from the belief in white racial superiority to the belief that white Americans are superior to all other whites.

White exceptionalism may only be overt in its racist formulation, but it remains covertly operative in much political discourse about the national exceptionalism of the United States.

Samuel Huntington, the late former Chair of the Harvard Academy for International and Area Studies, gave this form of white exceptionalism an exceptional academic credential. He argued that US democracy is based *uniquely* in "Anglo-Protestant culture," a specific group within the amalgam of whites, who constitute the "cultural core" of American identity and "the American creed" (2004, 18). In a book with the alarmist title, *Who Are We? The Challenges to America's National Identity*, Huntington explains that it was this Anglo-Protestant culture, alone, that produced, protected, and enshrined our democratic values, our individualism, our work ethic, and our commitment to the rule of law. Thus he thought it essential that immigrants who are not Anglo-Protestant assimilate and adapt, rather than influence or insist upon change. Huntington ignored the overwhelming evidence of the US as actually a syncretic culture – for example, in that the Founding Fathers borrowed the idea of federalism from the Iroquois Confederacy, that the US women's movement was inspired by women's political empowerment in native communities, or that the abolition and civil rights movements led by African Americans and other minorities were what really set this country on the road to democracy (see, e.g., Wagner, 1996, 2003; Okihiro 1994). These influences don't fit the imaginary white vanguardist narrative; hence they continue to be underreported and undertheorized.

Huntington is not an outlier. Examples abound of a level of fear and hostility, as well as guilt and uncertainty, toward the impending demographic shift in the United States, as if the country will simply not survive it. The right is making a full-scale effort to "take back our schools, our communities, and our nation" (Flanders 2010, 3). Public school curricula continue to be mangled in fights over whether the United States has what Stephen Colbert lampoons as "the greatest history in the history of History" (2012, 11). And though my main focus has been the United States (holder of the world's largest nuclear arsenal, lest we forget), the demographic dangers believed to be threatening white identity span every white-dominated part of the world. Derided political parties with Nazi sympathies are major players in many parts of Europe, and the swastika has come to be used to target not mainly or only Jews, but whatever immigrant groups are in the local vicinity. When we talk about the white imaginary, we are talking about a global phenomenon.

The question we must now turn to is whether an antiracist white exceptionalism provides an effective, or sufficient, rejoinder to the racist versions.

Antiracist White Exceptionalism

The desire for a post-racial future, and the desire that this come as soon as yesterday, may be driven for some by a Faulknerian pessimism. If whiteness will not harmonize, will not play nice with others, perhaps we must follow Noel Ignatiev and John Garvey's call to "give up on whiteness" (Ignatiev and Garvey 1996). After all, there is no doubt that the white imaginary is imbued with ideas of white supremacy, making whites feel entitled to dominance. It is not only the claim of being the *majority* (soon to be lost) that legitimates such entitlements, but the claim to *superiority*. Huntington's argument takes just this form: white majority rule was a good thing because white rule was a good thing. Majority status provides the alibi for the more deep-seated idea that whites should rule because whites rule best.

My principal concern with this form of white exceptionalism – the idea that whiteness is simply and irrevocably tied to supremacist illusions, that racism is the logos of whiteness – is that it assumes dubitable claims about the nature of social categories of identity and why they become adopted as self-ascriptions. It also assumes certain dubitable ideas about the meanings of concepts. And further, it makes assumptions about the stability and intransigence of racism itself and how, and where, it is configured on a map of social relations and structures. I will address each of these points in the remainder of this chapter, beginning with the question of how whiteness operates as a specific social identity in relation to white supremacy, before turning to the question of meaning, and then to the question of the stability, or instability, of racism.

The claim that whiteness is indelibly constituted by racism, that it cannot escape this past, is an empirical claim, of a sort. If the very concept of whiteness emerged at its moment of inception as a strategy to maintain the plutocracy by ensuring the allegiance of the European immigrant poor, and if whites have further been conscripted into participating, in one way or another, in the concomitant race-based colonialism unfolding in the same period, then, at the very least, the *meaning* of white identity will carry the connotation of this history. When one thinks of what it means to be white, or to *want* to be white, or to be *proud* of being white, one may perhaps conjure up many ideas, but one of these ideas will surely involve racial hierarchy. White southern US identity still carries a strong association with the Confederate States of America, despite the extremely brief tenure of the Confederacy, because of the long resistance to racial equality. The Confederate flag has become a well-recognized symbol of white southern identity, and arguments defending the flying of this flag on public lands invoke heritage claims, as if a disrespect for the Confederate flag is a disrespect for white southerners. But such craziness is not simply a semiotic chess match over disembodied symbols: plenty of southern white families, including my own, have passed down lore about the tribulations of family members during the Civil War, most of whom of course were not generals or colonels but suffering foot soldiers. Many African American families have lore as well about atrocities their families suffered at the hands of rural terrorists wielding this flag. The meaning of the Confederate flag is made manifest by these experiences.

The point here is that the rhetorical invocations of these histories, whether from politicians using white heritage or from antiracist activists, work as well as they do because they connect to real events and experiences. This is how the connotations of concepts and symbols are enlivened, and perpetuated. In a sense, one can agree with the heritage claims: yes, the Confederate flag does symbolize white identity in the sense that it denotes the myopic allegiances of too many of its individuals. But the concept of white identity, as with any construct of a social kind, also operates as a *belief* with *pragmatic outcomes on the future*. Ian Hacking (2000) uses the term "looping effects" to describe the ways in which our conceptualization and categorization of social phenomena, from racial identities to multiple personality syndrome, alter how people understand themselves and how this understanding affects their behavior. Looping effects can impact our interactions with the material world as well. To define "automobile" as a vehicle with an internal combustible engine that uses fossil fuels precludes the expansion of the concept, requiring "hybrid" or "electric" as a modifier, thus making these latter types stand out as odd. Why not take the more functional definition of the automobile as a motorized, covered vehicle for small occupancy transport, a definition that would encompass future inventions beyond what we can currently imagine? Problems occur not only when definitions are stubbornly held fast, but also when they are stretched for nefarious purposes, such as when the term "seed" is applied to genetically modified products that cannot in fact regenerate. I will say more about the issue of conceptual meanings in the next section, but it is vital to understand that terms constantly gather new connotations and applications, generating new debates and new boundaries. The point is to notice which boundaries we may be overstepping, whose experiences we are invoking, which feedback effects we may be generating, and what functions these may serve.

If we hold that white identity is essentially racist, we are surely circumscribing its future and generating distrust and antipathy toward all who so self-describe. We may then be disabling coalition and putting unnecessary brakes on the fluid alterations in people's self-understanding.

Whiteness is itself the manifestation of such alterable self-understandings. Before the Conquest, the widely variant groups in Europe did not coalesce under a racial identity. The myth of a unified lineage had yet to be born. The vast distances between English and Latin and Slav began to diminish only when the perspective of the "New" World created a common frame of reference in post-Conquest European thought (Dussel 1995). The high contrast with indigenous peoples of the Americas rendered the commonalities across warring European peoples more perspicuous (and the resultant colonial plunder rather effectively manufactured more commonalities). The etymology of whiteness reveals its grounding in these historical events that were engineered, perhaps, at the top, but experienced by the masses.

Just as importantly, the eventual development of a polyglot, multicolored working class in the societies bordering the Atlantic Ocean made cross-class white racial unity a useful idea for the white power elite. This mix of badly treated conscripts was not always docile, nor did they always prefer to fight amongst themselves rather than taking on their masters (Linebaugh and Rediker 2000). The concept of white identity emerged in the nineteenth century to take its familiar shape as an organizing frame for perception and behavior (Roediger 1991; Allen 2006). This conceptual development clearly benefited from the much longer tradition in Europe of associating whiteness with lightness, and lightness with being better, smarter, more moral, more beautiful, and more culturally advanced than darkness (Painter 2010). Yet to take hold in self-ascriptions, whiteness had to mean something, such as being correlated to employment advantage. As our economies change, then, the effective and material correlations of whiteness are shifting in ways that may already be changing its meaning. I will return to this point, but first we need to explore the question of meaning itself, and, in particular, whether the history of a concept determines its unending future.

The Historicism of Concepts, Or the Meaning Question

The Austrian philosopher Ludwig Wittgenstein held that the meaning of a word can only be based on the ways that real-world language users actually employ the word in a given time and place, rather than determined by the word's etymology or its interpretation by experts. An utterance containing a single word, "brick," can be correctly understood to refer to a gold brick, a clay brick, to be a shorthand way of saying "hand me a brick," or, more recently, it can be used as a slur, as in "dumb as a brick." We garner the word's specific meaning from the context of its immediate use. In fact, the meanings of a word often contradict its historical roots, which is why we find etymology so entertaining. Language use is endlessly inventive, and slang creatively mixes connotations to elucidate new sensibilities. Wittgenstein wanted to understand successful communication and found this to be rooted more in this lively lived practice than in a historical genealogy of authoritative interpreters.

Wittgenstein's use-based theory of meaning gains credence from the numerous concepts and terms that have radically changed meanings and connotations as social practices have evolved. The term "ethnic" used to be a synonym for "heathen," but today generally refers to cultural groups that share a certain lineage. The word "seduction" once stood in for the word "rape," though now these coercive associations have been dropped so that it means something like "enticement" or "temptation." The classical etymology of the word "philosophy" refers to the love of wisdom, an association scoffed at by most of the current profession.[1] Even the normative force of words can change from negative to neutral (as in the case of "ethnic"), and from positive to problematic (as in the case of "monarchy" or "divine right" or "pederasty"). In some cases all that changes is how we evaluate the practices to which the meanings refer, but in other cases, the uses themselves change and hence the meanings adjust. Consider the concept "marriage," which for a long time meant a rather cold, economic arrangement – one in which women were little more than hired breeders who ran households. In more contemporary times, the term has been romanticized (*ad nauseam*) to signify a consensual union based on mutuality and affection.

One can see from these examples how context, understood both temporally and spatially, is determinative over meaning. As José Medina (2006) has argued, building from both Wittgenstein and G. H. Mead, to connect meanings to use is necessarily to connect meanings to context. He argues further that "although meanings can only be *found* in contexts…they are not *contained* in contexts." There are always multiple contexts of use, none of which is completely fixed or closed. Hence, meanings "do not belong to the ontic domain of the physical or of the mental, but to the social and practical domain of the *interactional*" (2006, 50; emphasis in original).

What, then, of whiteness? Concepts such as whiteness refer to social kinds, bringing into play both empirical and pragmatic considerations. Whiteness is not some natural phenomenon we can only observe from a distance, nor is it a cultural trend like fashion, too mercurial to

---

1 See the controversy that beset Alain de Botton's (2001) claim that philosophy seeks wisdom. Anglo-American philosophers in particular define their vocation in terms of critical reason, and view "wisdom teaching" as insufficiently open to critique.

accommodate predictive graphs or meaningful correlations. We can map out the history of whiteness with some detail and we can also measure with some accuracy the present day economic and social benefits of having a white identity, or the "wages of whiteness," as it's called.

The uses of the term whiteness will make up a large and complex list, including laws, institutionalized forms of recognition, social advantages of various sorts, and learned (rather than natural) modes of interaction as well as the sort of interpretive judgments, perceptions, and affective responses as were discussed in Chapter 1. The latest US census stipulates a referential set for the category that ranges beyond those with European lineage to include people from the Middle East and North Africa, a usage at odds with other current uses, such as the self-ascriptions of such groups. The domain of real-world uses of the term is far from a neat or internally consistent set, and yet there are general patterns: white job and loan applicants continue to be judged more positively, and whites themselves have a specific set of measurable responses and perceptual habits that social psychologists have been cataloguing now for several decades (see, e.g., Steele 2010, Richeson and Trawalter 2008).

Whiteness studies itself has put into circulation new uses for the term. The distinguished sociologist of racism Joe R. Feagin (2013) has elaborated a concept he calls "the white racial frame" to signify an assortment of forms of racism that are systemic rather than individual. Charles Mills (2007) has developed the concept of "white ignorance" as a structural, group specific form of miscognition or willful unknowing. As David Owen puts it, rather severely, whiteness is a "structuring property of the social system," providing a "hierarchical ordering" of actions, practices, and values (2007a, 205–7). An example of the sort of structuring effects Owen has in mind is explained by Danielle Allen, who shows that even the *New York Times* business section operates with a whiteness standard: significant increases in the unemployment rates among nonwhites are treated as inconsequential when identifying economic upturns and downturns. The "common good" is measured in relation to whites (2004, 39–49).

These analyses bring into play invaluable new critical and analytical uses for the term whiteness by elucidating subtle aspects of the way in which white dominance is secured. Whether overtly stated or covertly implied, whiteness operates as the controlling term, the default position, the rightful majority, the most normal norm, and as such it demands a justifying explanation for any measure that attempts to unseat it or, for example, to make high unemployment figures for African Americans and Latinos a reason for dramatic policy shifts. Whiteness adds value, even when it is left implicit. Hence the term itself need not be used for it to be *in* use, so to speak.

The upshot of this new work is a new use for the term that can begin to appear pretty consistent, and consistently negative. Whiteness is, as Du Bois once said, a kind of "blind-spot." Yet we might wonder whether the *meaning* of whiteness is exhausted by these approaches that treat whiteness as a thing-like entity with predictable dispositions.

Despite our ability to describe whiteness as a structure and to measure with some precision its effects and associated practices, white social identity is not simply an objective thing, completely outside human agency, like Mars or the Milky Way. It is certainly not outside the collective agency of white people themselves. There is an associated "use" to the concept of whiteness, and it is here, in the variety and contextual multiplicity of this use, that we can discern best the possible openings for alterations.

Whiteness is a self-ascription for people with evolving (or devolving) practices and beliefs. It's a referring term used with varying intentions. Despite the close association of whiteness with racism, some white people have strenuously resisted racial hierarchies and have resented the unwanted entitlements, and concomitant burdens, of white privilege.

In his memoir of being a field organizer from the early days of the Student Nonviolent Coordinating Committee (SNCC), enduring constant arrests and a grim amount of violence, Bob Zellner (2008) recounts how he would remind his African American comrades when they would occasionally need to vent about whites and crackers that he was one of those as well. Occasional venting was vital given the regular brutality all the SNCC workers experienced, but, as a rural white kid from Alabama, Zellner never held himself apart from the rural terrorists they were fighting, except insofar as he had different moral and political commitments. He well knew the association Klansmen made between whiteness and supremacy, but he never declaimed being a white boy from lower Alabama, or "LA" as he later jokingly called it. Nor did he claim to be white in a way wholly different from the Klan, insisting that no one is entirely free of the racist society in which he or she is raised.

We should not be too quick to assume that a person's disidentification with supremacist ideas about whiteness entails a disidentification with whiteness itself. Zellner understood himself to be a rural white southern man, as well as a committed antiracist and, as he says, hopefully, at times, also simply a "human being." Neither the white power structure nor the Klan's context of use for the term "whiteness" fully determined the meaning of the term for Zellner, even though his family included Klan members and sympathizers and his social context was seriously affected by white supremacist ideas, social structures, and everyday practices.

Zellner's usage reveals a complex understanding of the connection between whiteness and racism. Racism is likely to be something every white must become reflexive about in order to overcome; a simple disavowal will never be sufficient. Yet to claim the term "cracker" while sitting in a southern jail for opposing antiblack racism works as a powerful disavowal of the necessary links between whiteness and racism.

Clearly, today's historical ferment is not unlike the heyday of civil rights. The demographic shifts, increasing level of social integration, growing movement for immigrant rights, and global power shifts are radically changing the social context in which the meaning of whiteness takes shape, particularly in regard to its association with supremacist ideas and who can be included in the referent class. The uses to which the term can be put are changing: whiteness can signify, similarly to the term "Aryan," as a kind of racist fabrication, or it can refer to a cultural lack or absence, or as an indicator of likely racism or racial ignorance, or as a metric of unearned advantage, or simply as a synonym for a person with some European (white) lineage. But the need for qualifications when "white" is taken to signify "European" indicates that we continue to need the term white in order to communicate. In truth, European American does not work as a synonym for white since then it would not be able to exclude Turkish Germans, Somali Italians, and English families who came from the Caribbean. To admit a fluidity of meaning opens the door for some to claim that Afro-Germans or Somali Italians are in some cases "culturally" white, but to call them white would still require an explanation of their relationship to the category that is unnecessary in the case of other Germans and Italians.

The context of use for whiteness has changed to such an extent that white identity can be a disadvantage in some specific situations, when a white person is a minority among other workers or other students with roughly comparable status in the workforce or classroom even though, of course, the reality of white dominance in the larger society always confers some positive status differential. As an illustration of this, Jonathan Lethem (2003) writes comically about his experiences growing up in the Gowanus neighborhood of Brooklyn as a minority white, at a time and place where his Jewish identity was not much of a factor. Being white played a definite role in the fact that he was daily "yoked" by classmates – "yoke" being the term for a headlock, the purpose of which was petty thievery. As Lethem tells the story, there was an element of camaraderie in the experience, with laughter and jokes about the repetitive and routine nature of the bullying. The potential for violence was checked, he suggests, by his status as one of the kids on the block rather than, for example, as a white interloper from Manhattan (who would have been coded as more privileged). Despite a certain degree of camaraderie born of the familiarity of sharing a school and neighborhood, Lethem was made by these classmates to feel the difference of his whiteness nonetheless, and not as a positive attribute.

Today, Lethem chalks the experience up as a life lesson about the limits of the ideals of colorblind race-neutrality. He explained that his hippie parents had evidently believed, like other overly optimistic white liberals at the time, that, by the 1970s, the social changes around race identity would be such as to have ensured a norm of colorblindness, so that their son Jonathan's status as a racial minority in the neighborhood school would not be an issue. Despite the fact that he chides his parents effectively for their naivety, Lethem also allows that it was his good fortune to grow up in a household that acknowledged the past prevalence of racism, since it was this that informed his own capacity to cultivate a certain patience toward his regular "yokes."

Lethem ends his story with this interesting commentary about his own subjective attitudes and experience, from hindsight:

> [I]t's worth saying that along with this level of pretentious, patronizing guilt and pity, another, more tender factor modulated the experience of being yoked/mugged. That was a kind of closeness in the act, its weird intimacy, its dailiness. We were in it together, like every bunch of miserable kids anywhere. We were making community and conversation, even if it cost me my bus pass every thirty days. Yeah, it was a difficult conversation – shouldn't it have been? The lives of the black kids around me meant

something to me, and I didn't only identify in a baroque and self-loathing way, but in a fine one as well. (2003, 104–5)

One of the points we might draw from this set of observations is that Lethem's identity as "white boy" was attached to a reality, not just an epithet imposing an illusory attribute (as might have been the case if they had called him "Christ-killer," for example). And yet his whiteness, and his awareness of his whiteness, did not preclude the possibility of an affective *rapprochement* in which a certain communal synchronicity was felt simultaneously to the mimed conflict. Lethem explains that this was in the early days of hip-hop, and "some of the other white boys being yoked in my neighborhood went on to become the Beastie Boys," assimilating, one imagines, their neighborly if tense camaraderie into an expressive form of cultural amalgamation (2003, 105). I suggest we need the category of whiteness to understand not only how Lethem's *objective positionality* worked in this social moment, how his opportunities and interactions were affected by it, but also to understand *his own reactions* to his experiences. Even while whiteness does not predict in any simple way, or exhaust, either his or the other kids' feelings about one another, we need the category to explain many aspects of these sorts of experiences.

The assumption that white privilege is legitimate is certainly undergoing an assault, and such instances of small-time aggression as Lethem describes may be a symptom of this. Long patterns of deference to whites finally began to diminish during the civil rights and Black Power movements. A newly felt empowerment for oppressed groups can feel heady enough to go overboard, and wonderful enough to scream out the window with a pair of loud car speakers. The fact that, as a kid, Lethem tolerated the aggression he experienced from his African American classmates was based in part on his own understanding of the legacy of unearned white privilege, as his liberal parents had educated him to grasp.

The overall lesson here is that how whiteness is lived, experienced, and understood is not a natural, unchangeable phenomenon. It has no essence unaffected by its context, nor is it so removed from our individual and collective agency that we can only sit back and watch it unfold. Decisions that whites make about where to live and where to go to school, as well as about how to live and how to interact with others, can change the real-world meaning, and the status, of whiteness.[1]

The question of the future meaning of whiteness should not be an attempt to predict so much as it is to argue, normatively, about what should be done. But, as Marx argued, the question of what *should* be done is constrained in turn by the scope of the feasible. So the point of a study of the present is not to game one's predictions of the future, but to ground one's normative arguments in realism.

The view I have elaborated thus far in this chapter can be summarized as follows: white exceptionalism, or the thesis that whiteness is so qualitatively distinct from other social identities that it can never mingle or harmonize, is based in a claim about the essential, and fixed, meaning of whiteness, and, in particular, its historical genealogy in white supremacy. The spotlight antiracists have placed on the category of whiteness has been helpful in revealing the ways in which white identity maintains dominance, even when not in overt use. The bottom line, however, is that meanings are determined by use, either overt or covert ones, and use is always specific to context. And contexts change.

---

1 It should go without saying that not all whites have options of where to live, such as Lethem's parents. The ability to choose one's neighborhood and school can obviously affect the resultant affective response to one's experiences there.

Finally, in the following section, I want to explore the question of racism's instability. How pessimistic should we be about racism's future?

The Instability of Racism

We have been throwing the term racism around with less care than we should have thus far. The term gets used in widely different ways in the media, in the academy, and in everyday speech, from a reference to individual prejudice or affect all the way to a focus on institutional outcomes. As Sullivan (2014) has powerfully argued, quite often the word conjures up images of working-class southern men as if these are the main perpetrators of the problem, leaving the rest of us to feel smugly safe from the need for self-reflection.

Philosophers have been arguing over how best to define racism for several decades, and, on the whole, most have aimed toward generalities, wanting a single coherent definition that covers all cases. The principal competing accounts in the philosophical literature today about the nature of racism concern whether racism is a belief (Piper 1992–3), a particular biological belief (Appiah 1992), a disposition toward exclusivist moral commitments (also Appiah 1992), or essentially an affective disposition (Garcia 1996). In other words, the debate is whether racism is a belief, a particular kind of belief, a failure of universalism, or an emotion. This is on the analytic or Anglo-American side of the discipline. Among continental philosophers – those who work in contemporary European philosophy – racism is often characterized as a form of negation or abjection of the Other, in which that Other is taken as something of a fungible generic. Among social theorists more generally, there has been a debate over whether racism can come under the all-enveloping concept of xenophobia to capture cross-historical and cross-cultural group hatreds of all forms.

There is an undoubted utility in approaches that try to develop a general account and that attempt to characterize the particular emotional attitudes and cognitive commitments that make up racism. Much of this work is motivated by the practical question of how we identify *when* racism has occurred. The cognitive view held that racism had to involve as a necessary condition some belief state that could be discerned in one's disposition and practice if not in one's conscious inventory of doxastic commitments. This seemed plausible, but others argued that it was overly intellectualist and neglected racism's emotional content. Racism, Garcia argued (1996), resides in the heart, and others, such as David Kim (1999), have taken up this idea to explore affects like disgust and repulsion as common features of racism. The intellectualist or cognitive characterization of racism is not well equipped to handle the fact that sometimes people persist in racism even when the erroneousness of their beliefs has been made abundantly clear.

The generalized approach to racism leads some to believe that all of its forms are traceable to a single cause, such as a fear of the foreign that evolved from human prehistory. *Hypotheses* by evolutionary psychologists about the group-functional character of out-group antipathy are often taken too quickly to establish *causal facts*; other scientists are countering with alternative hypotheses about natural altruism and the desire to mix.[1] The principal difficulty of applying naturalist approaches to racism is that the concept of race only emerges in the modern period. There were concepts about groups, and peoples, but it is not at all clear that such concepts were predicated on shared lineage or even shared visible phenotypes. Still, some try to take the broad concept of in-groups and out-groups, in which the way groups are formed is understood to be historically variable, and then tie evolutionary

---

1 For an overview of the criticisms of evolutionary psychology's hubris, see Rose and Rose 2000. For a more measured take, see Buller 2005.

explanations of this behavior to more recent social issues. I will discuss a case of this in my conclusion in relation to arguments by Glaser and Ryan (2013).

Darwin himself hypothesized on the basis of his varied observations that even while those individuals living on the edge of their colonies are exposed to more risk, and are literally unsettled, they are also those most likely to find new adaptations. Hence, living on the borders of what is foreign can serve to innovate the practices of a species, or group, enhancing its likely survival.

Jesse Prinz (2012) wrote, in effect, a rejoinder to determinist claims that make use of biology or brain studies – and this from someone who has done extensive work on cognitive science and the new neurosciences. Prinz wants to put the genome back in the bottle, as he puts it, to dispel the hype around genetic explanations for behavior. He emphasizes that there is simply too much human variety, diachronic and synchronic, to justify claims about a closed set of traits we might call human nature.

We should remember that difference can excite and attract as well as repel, and cultures intermingle peaceably far more often than they go to war (Said 2004). Many cities around the world, such as the one I live in today, take great pride in their array of multiple cultures, religions, ethnicities, racialized groups, nationalities, and linguistic identities who cohabit neighborhoods, schools, parks, and workplaces. In fact, such diversity is used as a major PR campaign, a moniker of the idea of urban living itself. Of course, there are hate crimes, but there are also long stretches of everyday life in which people mingle in the playgrounds and amicably share crowded public transportation. Natural disasters bring volunteers from one part of the city, traipsing into the effected areas with mops and shovels, and uncoerced cooperation springs forth in the face of more human-made atrocities, such as when a missing Jewish boy in Brooklyn brought Arabs and South Asians out to help their Orthodox Jewish neighbors circulate leaflets. Thus, let us not forget the low-intensity and quotidian bacchanal of much twenty-first-century living even as we explore and address the persistence of racism, racist wars, and racist political discourse. Let us also reflect on the exculpatory benefits of determinist claims.

Generalized abstract accounts that collapse multiple forms of racism into one all-purpose out-group antipathy are also in danger of merging widely disparate attitudes and histories. And general accounts have the further disadvantage of leading to one-size-fits-all remedies that remedy little, as a number of people have argued (Takagi 1992; Alcoff 2006). If some groups are derided as intellectual inferiors, others are stereotyped as clannish techno-nerds, and still others portrayed as violent fanatics, we need to recognize that racism can take the form of quite different emotions, from derision to disregard to fear. We will need correspondingly different avenues for redressing these significantly distinct forms of prejudice.

I suspect that another motivation for the generic approach to racism is the wish to avoid identity talk. Using terms like "the Foreign" and "the Other" can make us feel safely separate from the sphere of identity politics in any form. And, if we talk about the Other, we can avoid concretizing a particular historical group with its inevitable historical implications. Talk of generic racism implicates the human species; talk of antiblack racism implicates everyone who is not black.

In contrast to the generic approaches to theorizing racism, Lewis Gordon, building from the existentialist phenomenology of Jean-Paul Sartre, helped to inaugurate an in-depth analysis of antiblack racism as a specific phenomenon requiring its own analysis. In his first book, *Bad Faith and Antiblack Racism* (1995), Gordon used general Sartrean existential concepts such as the look, the facticity of the body, and the ideas of presence and absence. These are the very concepts that can be used to obviate distinctions and create a generic approach to intersubjective interactions, but Gordon used them as a basis for specific descriptions of the ways in which blackness is represented, and reacted to, in antiblack cultural contexts. For example, he analyzed the way in which black bodies exist in antiblack cultures as a kind of present absence, "a body without perspective" or a body without subjectivity (1995, 102). He further argued that blackness is a paradigm case of what Sartre called *de trop*, meant to signify the superfluity of existence, but with a specific meaning in regard to black people: the mere presence of a black body in certain places such as university classrooms is *de trop* in the sense that it requires explanation and justification in a way that a white presence does not.

Some of the experiential aspects of antiblack racism that Gordon describes might indeed prove widely applicable to other groups, while other aspects seem more specific to African Americans, such as the attribution of an a priori criminality. As Gordon puts it, criminality is so constitutive of the meaning of blackness in antiblack cultures that a black person is guilty until proven innocent. In this effort at a thick, contextual description of the specific historical conditions and set of cultural practices and discourses facing African Americans, Gordon brought forward the specific conditions of antiblack racism as a distinct phenomenon.

In my own view, racism is not a unified term with consistent implications. It attaches to specific and particular narratives of history, forms of knowledge, and forms of subjectivity with varied manifestations of desire and emotion. Gordon offers an astute analysis of forms of antiblack racism that manifest as love, as desire, and as attraction embedded within ideational notions of superiority and inferiority, explaining such phenomena discussed earlier in this chapter as the "love" professed for black people by pro-segregation southern whites.[1] His account

---

1 His analysis does not suggest that desire or attraction across difference is always a manifestation of essentialism and racism, however. His focus is on professions of love embedded within supremacist relationships in which the subjectivity of the other is treated as unnecessary, as when (sometimes) one loves one's pet precisely because it lacks the capacity for judging and interpreting one's behavior.

suggests the need to link cognitive and emotional accounts of racism, but does not imply a unified or static form.

I suggest we need to keep these complex constellations in focus against generic approaches that look past the specificities of racism's particular forms, deemphasizing their importance. By acknowledging racism's diversity and fluidity, we can be more attentive to its power to morph into new versions. Yet, if racism is so inherently diverse, how does the concept hold together? How can I justify calling a given phenomenon racist if I don't have a prior minimal understanding of what that involves?

Racism as I use the term involves a negative value or set of values projected as an essential or noncontingent attribute onto a group whose members are defined through genealogical connection – i.e., as sharing some origin – and who are demarcated on the basis of some visible phenotypic features. But this is not necessarily a belief, or an emotion, or an institutional outcome. Nor is the target of racism stable. Hence, the sort of general account I propose avoids privileging one motivation over another (e.g. belief or emotion), or one form over another (e.g. individual or institutional). The idea that racisms are complex constellations in specific contexts is an approach that will have a methodological payoff in mandating attentiveness to specificities rather than moving too quickly to ahistorical causal formations or generic explanations that don't explain much.

The variety of racist attributions cannot be boiled down to a single form that differs only in degree. There is no single emotion that might serve to unify the field of reactions between disdain, fear, distrust, indifference, and disregard. Pointing out that these are all negative is no help, since they engender quite different reactive behaviors. Indifference leads to neglect and *invisibilization*, while fear and distrust can lead to hypersurveillance. Some groups might be primarily despised, while other groups are primarily pitied.

What is at stake in this analysis is not only a more adequate understanding of racism, but also of the requirements of antiracist policies. Post-racialism, or a reduced focus on race, may seem to help with hypersurveillance, but it exacerbates the problem of *invisibilization*. Affirmative action does not help us address language prejudice. The move to emphasize standardized tests as opposed to the personal essay in college applications advantages some groups, since it avoids the identity cues that can trigger stereotyped interpretations (Takagi 1992). But standardized tests significantly hurt other groups of people who experience stereotype threats in such testing processes (Steele 2010). Hence, differences in the forms racism takes need different kinds of redress.

A more complicated understanding of the content of racism and its multiple forms helps us to see it sometimes where we may think it doesn't exist, but also may help us avoid reductive analyses that see it everywhere, in which every positive gesture is reduced to an essentialist assumption or self-interested motivation.

The point of claiming that racism is unstable is also to denaturalize its (possible) departure. Many believe that racism is an outdated ideology that will gradually lessen of its own accord until it finally disappears, like beliefs in witches or the practice of sun worshipping. The progressive changes we can sometimes witness across the generations of a family support this belief, as do aspects of our national histories. However, the belief that racism will wither away as the natural effect of improved education, communication, and the accelerated circulation of information also presumes a certain naturalness and rationality to its emergence in the first place. In other words, it assumes that racism arose as a natural effect of ignorance and fear, or from racial ideologies that are now losing their adherents, and that it will therefore simply die out as prejudice is slowly overcome.

Hence, to say that racism is unstable is to say that we can naturalize neither its appearance, its rise, nor its decline. If it is less a rational than a learned response to events, and if it involves an affectively motivated orientation toward our social world, we cannot cure it with information. Racism is not rational, but then, of course, neither are we.

Lawrence Hirschfeld's work provides an especially interesting case. His study of children's perception of human types provides evidence that children *learn* which visible features are relevant to human classifications (1996, 137). Previous researchers on race classification generally hypothesized the construction of racial categories as building from perception in a linear causal sequence. We see difference, and then we classify it. Hirschfeld's study shows that children come to see human beings as racial types only *after* they have successfully inculcated the dominant schemas of their specific social context.

Such research is helping us to reimagine the way the mind works. Rather than being like a general all-purpose problem solver, or simple computer, the mind is more like a "collection of... special-purpose tools, each targeting a specific problem or content" (Hirschfeld 1996, 12). Hirschfeld's experiments provide an empirical confirmation of the claims of philosophers from Mead to Heidegger to Merleau-Ponty that what we actually see represents the results of sedimented contextual knowledges. This is simply to say that "our individual sensibilities and perceptions are never purely individual, but are the result of our upbringing, heritage and identity" (Hirschfeld 1996, 137).

Hirschfeld's results may lead to overly hasty optimism about the possibility of change. If we set this research alongside the experiments developed by Claude Steele and others on identity and "stereotype threat," we can get a fuller picture. Steele has shown that

> our social identities can strongly affect things as important as our performances in the classroom and on standardized tests, our memory capacity, our athletic performance, the pressure we feel to prove ourselves, even the comfort level we have with people of different groups – all things we

typically think of as being determined by individual talents, motivations, and preferences. (2010, 4)

The effects of racial identity on one's behavior, intellectual performance, and social interactions are not entirely conscious, and may in fact contradict, and countermand, our conscious beliefs. Racism, too, is deep-seated, affecting our perceptual practices and judgments in ways that are hard to detect. Thus, both racial identity and racism are sedimented in core areas of human thought and activity, suggesting that changes will not occur easily. This raises questions about whether we can reasonably hope for change.

Yet, if racism is learned, we can try to teach a different lesson. And if the racial unconscious can be opened up for inspection and accountability, the human capacity for reflection might alter the specific constellation of sedimented practices of relationality, empathic identification, and general comportment with others that exists in a particular social context.

It remains true that the contingent character of racism also means that we need to see it as an ideology laying in wait, capable of appearing and increasing in intensity after it may seem to be long gone. Jews in Germany prior to the rise of the Nazis experienced the highest level of European acceptance any had experienced for hundreds of years – they attended university, could join the professions, becoming lawyers and doctors and professors (Pulzer 1992). There were no pogroms in Germany as there were throughout Ukraine, Lithuania, Belarus, and other countries further to the east. The relative acceptance of German Jews before the rise of the Nazis may have made it appear that anti-Semitism was withering away, but anti-Semitism, no less than racism, defies rational, self-interested explanations.

If racism is unstable, then neither a permanent fatalism nor a relaxed optimism is warranted. If it is not natural, then it is not inevitable but rather contingent and learned.

But it remains a powerful ideological response that can be mobilized anew, transformed, and redeployed in a new more palatable guise.

What To Do...

White exceptionalism precludes the project of asking what a realistic but progressive future might look like that included whites as whites, i.e. without deconstructing whiteness into class or ethnic identities. If, as I will argue in the following chapter, talk of a dissolution of whiteness is premature, then we need to consider an alternative. The complex and deep ways in which selves and social relations are constituted should counsel us to beware easy claims of transcending racism. So, what to do?

Let me return to the issue of white exceptionalism that I laid out in the beginning of this chapter. If white exceptionalism simply refers to the disanalogy that exists between whiteness and other racialized identities, given the ways in which whiteness is associated with imperial histories and cultural vanguardism, no matter how humble a particular family line may be, then this form of white exceptionalism is unobjectionable. White identity formation is distinct, no question.

However, if white exceptionalism refers to either of the two versions I gave above with the help of Newton and Goethe – that whiteness is the true universal (and thus justifiably the vanguard) or that whiteness is locked in opposition to people of color by its very nature – then I would argue that both should be rejected. Whiteness as a universal is obviously false, since whites are no more "race-less" than anyone else (Dick Gregory once scoffed at this idea when he said whites think they are "clear" people). The instability or contingency of racism should also counsel us to reject the claim that whiteness is necessarily oppositional, forever limited by its initial formulations. In reality, the meaning of concepts is dependent on elastic forms of practice and changeable contexts. The everyday concept of race is transmogrifying into something like ethnorace, vilified blackness has come to signify coolness and resistance and community, and *latinidad* and Nuyorican identities denote cultural and linguistic dexterity. Whiteness too might alter in ways we cannot yet imagine.

We still cannot analogize white identity with other ethnic and racialized identities. Its relationship to the imperial imaginary of the United States, its historical foundations in racism and cultural hierarchies, and its potential to provide an alibi for capitalist elites make whiteness truly distinct. So we need to retain a consciousness of its specific genealogy at the same time that we reject determinism about its political content. This might suggest a version of double consciousness different from Du Bois's original notion, but similar in its evocation of a set of conflicting, if not contradictory, features. Double consciousness for whites would mean strengthening the current effort to acknowledge the true history of white racism and imperialism, to continue to explore in detail the effects of that history on the constitution of whiteness and the white imaginary, as well as empirical realities of whiteness that are often mistakenly characterized as a simple meritocracy. Simultaneous to this ongoing exploration, double consciousness for whites would also seek to uncover the hidden histories of white antiracist resistances and the possibilities these histories may hold for new ways to be in the world and with others.

I would not argue, however, that we can look to the rational interests of the majority of whites to find the means to win them over to the fight against racism. Whites' rational interests are subject to a racist configuration, as I've argued, and antiracism is no more stable than racism.

Yet multiracial, multiethnic political coalitions exist all around us, from Occupy movements to the struggle to end police violence to the fight for the dignity of immigrants to daily labor struggles. What we lack, however, is a new imaginary or narrative that can make sense of the white participation in these new racially conscious counter-publics. One can sometimes see a groping toward this among the armies of white progressives in antiracist struggles who cannot quite articulate why they are in the room. The liberal language of transcending race is sometimes the only one they have available. But I will argue in the following chapter that an effective double consciousness refuses the transcendence of race consciousness or of one's white identity. An effective antiracism cannot be rooted in avoiding race but in an awareness and acknowledgment of its power.

The idea of a white double consciousness has two aspects: that whites are affected by racist histories and also by everyday amiable connections and affective pulls across racial lines.

James Baldwin recounts a local leader of the civil rights movement in Tallahassee, Florida explaining a related idea in 1960 as they sat together in a segregated hotel. The man's name was Richard Haley, a faculty member at Florida A&M University (FAMU) who later lost his job because of his role in the struggle. But that night he explained to Baldwin how the movement was built on the belief that the conscience of white people – even southerners, even redneck southerners – could be awakened. Baldwin asks Mr. Haley:

> [W]hat, in his judgment, is the attitude of most white people in the south. I confess myself baffled. Haley doesn't answer my question directly. "What we're trying to do," he tells me, "is to sting their consciences a little. They don't want to think about it. Well, we must make them think about it. When they come home from work," Haley continues, "and turn on the TV sets and there *you* are – " he means *you* the Negro – "on your way to jail again, and they know, at the bottom of their hearts, that it's not because you've done anything wrong – something happens in them, something's got to happen in them. They're human beings too, you know." (Baldwin 1985, 226–7)

Baldwin adds, "and in spades." This monumental charity is something we might learn from.

Compare Haley's non-exceptionalist view of whites to that of Faulkner. Antiracist whites and resistant blacks in his novels are lynched, turned on by their communities, murdered, and beheaded. Their family members bury them and then conceal all evidence of their gravesite for fear that white racists will dig up their corpses and bugger them anew. Faulkner can imagine antiracist whites – he himself was one, to an extent – but he cannot imagine a different south, or a different country, in which the broad dimensions of moral communitarianism are redrawn in more inclusive ways.

Small Revolutions

Less than two decades after Richard Haley was being interviewed by Baldwin in Tallahassee, the Ku Klux Klan successfully petitioned the town council to allow a public march. So began my stint as an anti-Klan activist. We organized students over at the majority white campus of Florida State University, my campus, to join with the students from FAMU, as well as numerous community and church groups, to counter the Klan's march with a little demonstration of our own. We hoped to create a large multiracial "unwelcoming" committee as the Klan marched through Tallahassee.

Not everyone who was opposed to the Klan wanted a public event. The prevailing strategy during this period was to ignore the Klan, to let them have their little marches, and to stay away so as to avoid helping them garner more publicity. But we were young hotheads, incensed by the fact that the Klan used their marches to raise funds, spread lies, and gather recruits. And our proposal for a counter-demonstration met with strong enthusiasm on the campuses and in the community. We took precautions to avoid any kind of incident that might get someone hurt (who didn't deserve to be). The Tallahassee police were in bed with the Klan and would have been happy to sabotage our fragile coalition, so our friends who could pass most easily as rednecks infiltrated around town to scout out trouble.

On the day of the march, there were so many Klan-haters in the streets that the Klan's intended route had to be rather rapidly and haphazardly cut short. The police hurriedly pushed robed Klansmen into vans – vans that they had hoped to use to arrest us – in order to protect them from the angry multiracial crowd, some of whom had bricks. We felt incredibly elated, but our elation was cut short that same evening as threats of reprisal reverberated through the community.

The rural South of the 1970s and '80s was ruled by the Klan. In rural southwest Georgia, shortly before our event, a white woman with a black lover was chained to a tree and beaten with a whip. But the cities were not immune from Klan activity either. Four black women in Chattanooga, Tennessee, were shot by white racist "joyriders." At Georgia State University in the heart of Atlanta we regularly found recruitment leaflets placed by Klansmen in library books. Despite a long record of racist violence, the Klan applied for and received permits to march in towns and cities across the South.

To counter their power, anti-Klan activists mostly used the tactics of small-scale organizing. We used alternative presses to publicize the truth about their activities and built networks of antiracist southern campuses. We also looked for opportunities to reach the white poor with a different message. The work was dangerous. Over the next several years I had friends were who shot at and dragged out of their cars or pistol whipped and left for dead in a ditch on rural roads in the middle of the night. A close comrade was raped by Klansmen in fields across from her home because she had publicly taken a lead in multiracial labor struggles. Another good friend had infiltrated Klan rallies to gather evidence but was discovered and seriously beaten. Some of these friends were not white, some were not white but could pass, and some were white. I myself was threatened by goons more than once, and learned to shoot (sort of).

We always went to anti-Klan rallies with cars carefully stripped of any political bumper stickers or other telltale signs. We made sure to have tanks full of gas so we wouldn't need to fill up in a rural area. We drove between cities in car pools. Sometimes we went armed.

The major cities of the South were mostly safe from open Klan violence, but everyone knew that to travel between cities, between Atlanta and Birmingham, for instance, one was on one's own. Local police departments were full of sympathizers as well as outright Klansmen, and one could get stopped under any pretense. Black people did not often travel at night, and black and white people traveling together did so at their peril even during the day. A mixed group of such anti-Klan activists driving together, in my borrowed car, were stopped, taken to police headquarters, separated, questioned, and charged with bogus crimes. Ironically, the charge was white slavery, since one person was under the age of 18 and was traveling across state lines.

Two years after our heady success in Tallahassee, five antiracist activists, some of whom were members of the Communist Workers Party (CWP), were openly murdered in broad daylight in the parking lot of a housing project in Greensboro, North Carolina (Bermanzohn and Bermanzohn 1980). Despite the fact that some southern newspapers painted the victims as extremists who all but incited their own murders, many across the South took this massacre as a sign that things had to stop. Although I was not a member of the CWP, their bold murders were a tragedy that had reverberating implications for the work we were trying to do. We took the national publicity the murders engendered as an opportunity for an even bigger organizing effort, and created the Southern Student Activist Network to link student efforts across campuses from Georgia and the Carolinas all the way to Virginia. We also created the Anti-Klan Network to coalesce community efforts to publicize and stop Klan violence. Within months of the murders, we put together a major march in Greensboro itself to showcase this cross-racial condemnation of the Klan. I rode home to Atlanta from that march late at night in my designated car pool, flying down the dark highway as fast as my old Dodge Dart could go to keep up with the others. We didn't worry about getting stopped for speeding; if police had tried to pull us over, our plan was to speed up and keep going.

Three women friends carpooling home from an anti-Klan march in Alabama that year were shot at while assailants attempted to force their car off the road. As soon as they saw the roadblock, the one black woman in the car quickly lay down on the floor to stay out of sight, while one of the white women got out her pistol, but the driver skillfully maneuvered the car off the road, around the Klansmen, and then back onto the road beyond their roadblock. The car in front of them, with two men in it, had been pulled over, but the women knew it was useless for them to try and stop to help. Those men, both white, were hospitalized for severe beatings they took that night.

Although it was important that our work against Klan violence was pursued through cross-racial coalitions, the main struggle, we knew, was within white communities. There was no need to knock on doors in black neighborhoods to convince people the Klan was a problem. Those of us working in poor white communities in the South discussed and debated, and sometimes strongly disagreed, about strategy. How could we simply bring an anti-Klan message to these poor beleaguered communities? How could we urge them to support other communities without in any way addressing their own problems? They experienced real poverty too. I stayed with a local family during one organizing drive in a famously poor white neighborhood of Atlanta, known as Cabbage Town. My hosts, Jonny and Gail, put me up in the bedroom of their teenage daughter, where there was a sort of shrine to Elvis fashioned on top of the dresser. For breakfast meat, Gail sliced hot dogs lengthwise to resemble bacon. A 20-pound plastic container of lard, an off-brand version of the Crisco I'd grown up with, and large enough to be restaurant-sized, stayed put in her kitchen next to the stove, dipped into for every meal. Gail and Jonny were absolutely salt of the earth, without much of any sort of formal education. They were poor, cheerful, and completely clear-eyed about the social hierarchies that put them on the bottom. They knew who ran the country and in whose interests, and they were resolutely antiracist. Except for their politics, they reminded me of my own family.

In 1977 we were organizing in Cabbage Town in response to the police murder of Bennie McQurter, a 26-year-old white Vietnam veteran who had been yanked out of a local bar by the cops for no greater crime than being drunk. In front of his friends and neighbors, McQurter was put in a chokehold and killed. He died in the middle of the street, in the neighborhood he grew up in, at the hands of white cops. This is the sort of everyday institutional violence some think is exclusive to black and brown communities, but unnecessarily rough and punitive responses from authorities happen routinely to poor whites. We hoped that by organizing a big campaign around McQurter we could make inroads toward a white–nonwhite coalition around police treatment, poverty, and class-based injustices. Thus, instead of just taking an anti-Klan message to Cabbage Town, we tried organizing around problems they shared with African Americans, and building a coalition from there. The campaign actually worked pretty well; in hindsight I'd say the limitations came from our own organization, not the organizing plan. We were young.[1]

---

1 Just to fill out this story, I worked in alliance with varying groups with people from varying classes and races, most of whom were southerners. Today, nearly to a person, the hundreds of people I worked with from back then are labor organizers, community organizers, housing activists, radical academics and journalists, and lawyers and progressive elected officials. *La lucha continua.*

Antiracist activity among white workers, as well as cross-racial alliances around labor, housing, prisons, and police violence, is occurring all over the United States today, from Ferguson to Oakland to Brooklyn. There is quite a long history of this, despite periods of ebbs and flows. It is not exceptional. Most of the struggles are local, and most are all but ignored by the mainstream press. No success is stable: although the Klan's power in the South was effectively undercut by the 1990s through a combination of legal maneuvers and organizing, neo-Nazi groups are mushrooming today all over the United States with help from social media. But success has to be measured by the experiences people have in working together in new ways, in new combinations. Those experiences alter one's sense of oneself and one's community in a way that can be permanent.

– 3 –

Double Consciousness

The most trenchant observers of the scene in the South, those who are embattled there, feel that the southern mobs are not an expression of the southern majority will. Their impression is that these mobs fill, so to speak, a moral vacuum and that the people who form these mobs would be very happy to be released from their pain, and their ignorance, if someone arrived to show them the way. I would be inclined to agree with this, simply from what we know of human nature. It is not my impression that people wish to become worse; they really wish to become better but very often do not know how.

James Baldwin, *The Price of the Ticket*, 1985

Baldwin was not always as optimistic as this passage, written during the early 1960s, might suggest. And southern activists such as Bob Zellner, who served as the white Field Secretary for SNCC during the same period as Baldwin was writing this passage, was not this optimistic either about the white mobs, who wanted nothing better than to string both him and Baldwin up to the nearest tree. Baldwin's comment was written, interestingly, just as he was touring the South and watching the struggle for civil rights unfold before his eyes. He penned these words even

as he was seeing the dialectic play-out between the out-
landishly brutal – and state-organized – repression against
the movement and the brave and smart young social revolutionaries spreading out with determination across the
black belt. For that is what the civil rights activists were:
revolutionaries. No other word can capture the spirit of
people willing to risk everything, including their lives, to
force change in the Old South, from the bottom up.

Today, many look at this history with a jaundiced eye.
From the luxury, and safety, of hindsight, we judge these
battles over the integration of public facilities against the
frustrating persistence, a half century later, of poverty and
unemployment and substandard housing and police violence and the ballooning prison complex. Even the civil
rights movement's successes with regard to the vote and
the removal of literacy tests have simply led to more wily
mechanisms that thwart the electoral power of people of
color through permanently disenfranchising convicted
felons and inventing new and inhibiting requirements at
the polls, ostensibly to thwart voter fraud.

Few can deny that the social situation of African Americans in the United States today remains shocking for such
a rich country. Yet too many of us, from all backgrounds,
have grown accustomed to this state of things, viewing its
familiar everydayness as no more remarkable than the sun
coming up. It is of course true that there is now a larger
black middle class, but the percentages of poverty, including child poverty, in the community that traces its lineage
to slavery should shame this country, and the fact that it
does not should shame it even more.

Shame is, however, a painful emotion. One wants to
avoid it, or avoid thinking about it. It seems to debilitate
thoughtful agency and productive action, forcing an
inward focus rather than on what needs to be done. Nonetheless, some white theorists have argued that shame and
guilt are legitimate and understandable reactions and can
even provide effective motivations. Sandra Bartky, for
example, disagrees with the "conviction of the American

Left" that guilt is politically demobilizing (2002, 134). In her view, guilt is the understandable result of realizing that one benefits from unearned advantages, that one's peaceful and prosperous life is made possible by structural violations against the dignity and needs of vulnerable groups, both locally and internationally. Guilt is a fact caused by one's social location in such a structure, and though defensiveness may be a common first response to charges of guilt (as she often sees in her middle-class students), there are other possible reactions. Like Bartky, I regularly see students disturbed by how ignorant they have been, angry at their educations, and developing new "feelings of solidarity with the victims of injustice" (Bartky 2002, 135). Dan Haggerty, who, like Bartky, is a philosopher of moral psychology, takes on the more difficult emotion: shame. He argues that, although shame can engender "vicious anger" and "narcissistic rage," it can also, like guilt, motivate us "to try to reconnect, to work for forgiveness and reconciliation" (2009, 304). The anger that shame and guilt evoke is justified and can be politically productive when directed toward the real causes of our unwitting complicity. These philosophical analyses gain further elaboration from a growing number of memoirs and biographies of white activists who show the mobilizing effect of these difficult emotions (e.g. Pratt 1991; Fosl 2002; Malan 1990; DeWolf and Morgan 2012).

Simone de Beauvoir's memoir (2000) of visiting the United States for the first time in 1947 is interesting in this context. Beauvoir spent four months lecturing and touring across the country, and, though many parts of the culture animated her interest, the differences between and relations among whites, blacks, Latinos, and Native Americans were a central chord in the subsequent observations she published. Some of these observations clearly stereotype racial differences: for example, when she describes "puritan" whites and "sensual" blacks (2000, 38). But she also astutely described the intensity of racism in Jim Crow America, the hypocrisies of urban sophisticated white liberals, and the effects of living in a racist society on white subjective life. These experiences, especially her visits to Harlem and New Mexico, instigated Beauvoir's own self-examination. As she recounts experiences of shame or deep-seated discomfort, she was not simply commenting on the racism of others, but awakening to the deep and complicated nature of her own white subjectivity.

Socializing with Richard Wright in the Jim Crow New York of the 1940s, Beauvoir notes the hostile glances and feels herself "stiffen with a bad conscience" (2000, 37). She observes:

> Harlem weighs on the conscience of whites like original sin on a Christian. Among men of his own race, the [white] American embraces a dream of good humor, benevolence and friendship. He even puts his virtues into practice. But they die on the borders of Harlem. The average American, so concerned with being in harmony with the world and himself, knows that beyond these borders he takes on the hated face of the oppressor, the enemy... He feels hated; he knows he is hateful... And all whites who do not have the courage to desire brotherhood try to deny this rupture in the heart of their own city; they try to deny Harlem, to forget it. It's not a threat to the future; it's a wound in the present, a cursed city, the city where they are cursed... And because I'm white, whatever I think and say or do, this curse weighs on me as well. I dare not smile at the children in the squares; I don't feel I have the right to stroll in the streets where the color of my eyes signifies injustice, arrogance, and hatred. (2000, 36)

Individual antiracist intentions count for naught in a social realm overdetermined by histories of slavery, lynching, and sanctioned racism. A smiling white face would signify condescension, or hypocrisy, in a society where shared water fountains constituted the threat of pollution. Beauvoir rightly notes that whites knew, even then, that there were double standards for civility, justice, and benevolence. Many recognized that the platitudes of national moral superiority were so hollow as to be cruel. As a result, she opines, the white person who enters a space like Harlem "feels hated; he knows he is hateful." His or her true reason for avoiding the area is not crime, but the psychic discomfort of guilt.

Here, then, we have the beginnings of a conception of white double consciousness, as I shall develop it in this chapter. Du Bois introduced the idea of double consciousness to describe the psychic situation of oppressed groups who see themselves through two sets of eyes: their own and their oppressors. For whites, or any dominant group, double consciousness involves coming to see themselves through both the dominant and the nondominant lens, and recognizing the latter as a critical corrective truth. In other words, one comes to recognize that colonialism, genocide, slavery, and the ongoing practices of white supremacy, as Du Bois so forcefully put it, are not instances of "Europe gone mad" but of Europe itself, "the real soul of white culture... stripped and visible today" (Du Bois 1986, 929). Coming to terms with the long and persistent legacy of this history requires coming to terms with whiteness.

Coming to terms requires courage. Studying African American, Native American, Chinese, Chicano, or Puerto Rican history, touring a museum with a slavery exhibit, or visiting three prisons in Louisiana, as the Arkansas born poet C.D. Wright recounts, produces troubling emotions, even in anticipation. She writes:

> I already feel guilty.
> I haven't done anything.
> But I allow the mental pull in both directions.

She recognizes both the smallness of this act, as well as its importance:

> It is an almost imperceptible gesture, a flick of the con-
> science, to go, to see, but I will be wakeful.
> It is a summons. (Wright 2007, xv)

Avoidance, Denial, Shame

Even just a discussion of white identity produces troubling anticipation. Lawrence Blum's (2012) plan to teach a course on race and racism in a highly diverse high-school classroom was beset with apprehension, from others as well as himself, about how the white students might respond, and what the nonwhite students might say. Many theorists and politics watchers take whites' reluctance "to go, to see" as an indication that a discussion of race in general, much less whiteness, is simply a nonstarter for social change. The fact that shame and guilt linger in the background of any talk about whiteness plays a debilitating role in getting discussions off the ground. "The question of who is to blame" for the racial dimensions of poverty in the United States "is a major fault line of American politics," Jack Turner correctly asserts (2012, 3). He sees the split in public opinion over how to address poverty as the result of blame-avoidance strategies. In particular, he argues, our celebrated "American" individualism, with its repudiation of structural explanations for poverty, is powerfully motivated by this desire to declare ourselves as individuals separable from history and structure. Our political values and even our social ontologies are motivated by a determination to avoid, or assign, blame.

There is no doubt that the reason the topic of whiteness and white identity rarely comes up is because of a fear it will lead to talk of blame and shame. Political operatives warn politicians to avoid such topics, with the ironic result that white male workers as a group have been left high and dry by the Democratic Party (see, e.g., Glaser and Ryan 2013; Haney-López 2014). Electoral strategists believe that appealing to such voters would require adopting one or other of two bad tactics: either accommodating the racism one will undoubtedly find in this cohort, or actually challenging it. The first strategy would compromise the Democratic Party and the second would likely fail. As a result, most public discourses generated by elections avoid the topic of race, whiteness, and the country's racial future.[1]

In truth, the desire to avoid whiteness-talk exists on both the left and the right, though the avoidance takes different forms. The right assumes that an analytical approach to whiteness will soon get around to talk of blame, and that any talk of blame is unfounded and based only in resentment or opportunism. They are willing to talk about whiteness, but only in terms of an aggrieved and blameless constituency. In this chapter, I will once again ignore the right in order to focus instead on the more interesting left-wing version of avoidance, in its guise as a proposal for the "elimination" of white identity. I will borrow here a term philosophers use in metaphysics debates – "eliminativism." As awkward as the term sounds, it helpfully underscores that this tendency is an "ism" – a theoretical disposition with political motives.

What role does the idea of whiteness itself – not white racism, but simply white identity – play in the construction and proliferation of racism and social dysfunction? Some argue it is the key problem, and because it is the key problem, whiteness – in the sense of people thinking they are white – stands in the way of social progress. Because white workers have been led to think of themselves as white, to develop a "sense of whiteness," as Roediger puts it, they are led to disidentify with non-white workers and believe they have some indelible connection to the billionaire class (Roediger 1991, 8; see also Allen 2006). In a related argument, some hold that the problem is that *racial* identifications have come to dominate *group* identifications, thus producing a dysfunctional race-based group-think that organizes and motivates oppositional thinking.

Group conflict theory is based on experiments going back to the 1950s that demonstrate how self-interest can

---

1 This is not meant to imply that the Democrats or liberals in general forgo covert appeals to white racism. Alas, all too often.

be organized into group categories along an apparently arbitrary set of markers, such as teams at summer camp that are demarcated simply by being given different names (see, e.g., Sherif 1956; Tajfel et al. 1971). The idea is that, while oppositional behavior may be hard-wired from our long evolution, the mark used to identify the relevant opposition group is intensely malleable and subject to suggestion. In Muzafer Sherif's classic psychological experiment, violent hostility between groups of boys at a summer camp was animated by no more than a few days' bonding experience and the creation of distinguishing group names: in this case, the "Rattlers" versus the "Eagles." All were Protestant, white, and middle class, and had moreover been screened to ensure that they were "well adjusted." Hence, the researchers' capacity to generate group-based hatred and violence so quickly and easily among this homogeneous assemblage took them by surprise (Glaser and Ryan 2013, 14–20).

Applying this analysis to whiteness may seem to lend support for eliminativism. If we could just convince white people to stop thinking of themselves as white, or at least to downplay this race-based way of thinking about social dynamics, we could make more effective political coalitions across these problematic categorizations. How plausible is such a strategy?

Ethnicity Instead of Race?

If whites are to downplay their racial identification, how should they identify themselves instead? As the stand-up comic Hari Kondabalu jokes, when he asks white people about their identity he gets a "math equation" – varied percentages of European ethnicities, with the ubiquitous Native American thrown in. This indicates that it is *already* the case that whiteness is not uppermost in their minds. At least, their conscious minds.

Still, perhaps the ethnic fractions that make up such math equations as Kondabalu hears could replace the all-purpose, and all-important, whiteness that disables class-based political coalitions. The project of eliminativism could then take advantage of the practice already common among whites to view other features of their lineage as more important than their whiteness.

But these ethnic histories are in many cases, as Mary Waters (1990) has put it, "options" that whites can take up or leave off as they please, since they are no longer meaningful aspects of their everyday present. Waters's characterization of white ethnic identity as optional is certainly not true for all whites, since some have had robust and continuous ethnic identities since their immigration, which can be pretty recent, as in the previous year. But Waters's claim is certainly true for many whites whose ethnic ties are all in the distant past and are indeed sufficiently complex to require, in truth, a math equation.

Importantly, thinking of oneself as white does not conflict with claiming such ethnic lineages. In fact, ethnic lineages provide proof of one's whiteness, and can be used in precisely this way by ambiguous-looking folks who may be taken for something else. One might want to argue (as I would) that, in reality, having French relatives does not establish one's racial identity, and yet we know that in real-world uses of European national and ethnic monikers, white identity is an unstated assumption. This is so universal that it requires no explanation in usual contexts, where someone, by contrast, with darker skin or indigenous features who claims to be French may get questions.

It is certainly true that stating one's ethnic lineage is not generally used to establish one's whiteness: it can also be relevant, as I argued in Chapter 1, to one's present day life and family. Having Irish forebears may explain why some family members are police officers, but one will need more than an ethnic category to explain why the contemporary generation of one's family has been able to integrate into more well-paying sectors of the labor market. Being Irish signals that one is white, but each term yields a different explanatory value.

Our social identities are made up of many elements, some perfectly consistent with each other (such as being Scottish and white) while others are in tension (such as being Arab and white). Despite these variations, being classified and viewed as white, even if only on the margins of the category, is hardly insubstantial. As a social category of identity, then, whiteness continues to have explanatory value, to inform our hermeneutic horizons and ways of being in the world, and to be a part of our collective material culture. Eliminating the term, or even the self-ascription, does not eliminate the thing, no matter how complex and changeable that thing is. As Howard Winant puts it:

> [Whiteness is not so] flimsy that it can be repudiated by a mere act of political will…[it is] an overdetermined political and cultural identity nevertheless, having to do with socioeconomic status, religious affiliation, ideologies of individualism, opportunity, and citizenship, nationalism, etc.…; rather than trying to repudiate it, we shall have to rearticulate it. (1997, 48)

The only real way for whiteness to cease being a fit manner of identification would be to transform the conditions – material, cultural, political, and economic – that make it operative and explanatory. But even here my sense of the power of history makes me skeptical.

The project to rearticulate whiteness needs to begin with a better understanding of its history. Interestingly, the recent historical accounts about those derided southern Europeans who managed after some decades to become accepted as white, and thus free from state-sanctioned social exclusions in housing, education, and social clubs, can hold a clue to the possibility of such transformation as Winant calls for. As Ellen K. Feder and others have shown, outlying groups were able to become white not simply when the state began to disallow such practices as Irish exclusions, but also by a set of positive practices intentionally inculcated among the designated groups (Gans 1967; Feder 2007). It was possible to become white, but, at least for some, this took a certain amount of work. The founder of Levittown believed that

> [E]thnic Europeans could be "made white" as a result of the entitlements afforded returning GIs. "Becoming white" on Levitt's terms entailed molding a kind of suburban lifestyle whereby habits that typified immigrant city life were "corrected" via rulebooks distributed as homeowners' manuals. That the first houses in Levittown were available for rent with the option to buy only after a year signals the consequences of a failure to conform to the expectations specified in the manual, namely eviction. (Feder 2007, 33)

These manuals – which were, as Feder points out, textbook examples of Foucauldian disciplinary practices – included edicts about cleanliness and orderliness as demonstrable in the condition of one's yard and one's children. The spatial organization of each home, as well as the neighborhoods, assumed and reinforced normative gendered divisions of labor, with wives in kitchens overlooking the yards where children played, while husbands had space for "do-it yourself" projects in their basements. Outdoor clotheslines were prohibited, and homeowners were subject to supervision of their lawn-care for the first several years. Neighborly proximity encouraged compliance through a panoptic oversight. The political implications of all this discipline were not lost on its proponents: Levitt himself was of the opinion that "No man who owns his own house and lot can be a communist. He has too much to do" (Feder 2007, 36).

Today's modern gated communities and condos have lists of rules not totally dissimilar from Levitt's edicts. My own condo in Brooklyn disallows doormats outside apartments and all home decorating projects are subject to board approval. Neighborhoods marked by "historic preservation" rules similarly restrict both structural and cosmetic changes, policing even the color one can paint one's house. These rules sometimes beset newly gentrifying neighborhoods, helping to push nonwhite homeowners out who cannot afford the practices demanded by vigilant preservationist committees. Many workplaces have found ways to discourage styles of dress that signify as working class or nonwhite, and the grooming practices expected in many professions are both onerously expensive and ethnocentric.

Thus, we have not entirely left behind the enforced normalizing practices that we must accede to in order to maintain middle-class life, and these are always about race as well as class. Levittown *required* racial discrimination as an overt condition of sale, and Levitt justified such rules on the grounds of economic "realities" that would disadvantage all the homeowners if housing stock dropped due to integration. Today's neighborhoods, gated communities, and condo and coop associations can no longer overtly discriminate; many are diverse and some are even majority–minority, such as the numerous Latino enclaves in the booming gated communities of south Florida. Still, today's real estate realities have not changed much. "Loud" colors, folk art yard ornaments, and unkempt lawns are still policed in a manner that reminds us of older efforts to inculcate non-WASP whites into WASP ways. The specter of a normative, northern European, waspy whiteness still dominates the aesthetic signs of middle-class success.

Yet, the very fact that whiteness depends on practices reveals its vulnerability. Whiteness is undoubtedly an objective social location within macro social structures that confer differential advantages, and it is also a visible phenotype whose semiotic connotations are beyond individual control. But white identity is also manifest in how one conducts one's life. Breaking the rules may not change people's racial identity, but can it rearticulate the meaning of whiteness? Can rearticulation merge into elimination? Before we can tackle these questions, we need to look more thoroughly at the eliminativist option. An effective rearticulation of whiteness should be wary, so I shall argue, of the temptations of eliminativism.

Left-Wing Post-Racialism

Right-wing post-racialism, as opposed to left-wing post-racialism, is a form of eliminativism focused on the denial of racism. As David Theo Goldberg puts it, this "widespread view, especially among white Americans, is that racism would disappear if everyone simply ceased making (so much of) racial references" (1997, 9). People of color and white liberals are charged with overinflating the problem of racism motivated by their own paranoia, resentments, and fixation on the past. This version of the post-racial call is without enough argumentative merit to take seriously: certainly, they are correct that paranoia and resentments exist among some, but the bald realities of white dominance in economic and political power prove that race-*talk* is not the problem (Hacker 2003; Oliver and Shapiro 1997). In fact, most of the paranoia and resentment that disable our public spheres are those manifest among whites, as Tim Wise's work (2012) so patiently and perceptively demonstrates.

But we need to be clear that post-racialism is not simply a delusion of the right. There is a left-wing version of post-racialism as well. This version may apply post-racialism to whites only, or to whites first, on the grounds that white identity is less "real" because it was so obviously a manipulation from the top. But it may also incorporate the call to end the use of the term whiteness within an overarching proposal to reject all racial terms, *tout court*. Or, it may be based on the claim that the meaningfulness of whiteness, along with other gross group categories, is on the wane as social identities of all sorts become increasingly fragmented, fluid, and overlapping.

We might, then, divide the left-wing eliminativists into three broad camps. The first camp is primarily motivated by a commitment to end white supremacy. They argue that whiteness is a dangerous illusion to which we should become, as it were, traitors, as both a practical and an ideological project. The second camp is motivated by the idea that the category "race" is just too conceptually and politically problematic to be maintained in any form, because of either its biological implications, or its association with racism and exacerbation of "group-think," or the dangerous misuses to which the concept might be put, and so on. The third camp is motivated by a sense that whiteness is on its way out: because the political orientation among whites is no longer as united as it once was, because the boundaries are down, and because who gets to count as white has become less clear cut.

In this final chapter I hope to put this "eliminativist" option to rest. Motivations aside, the terms "race" and "whiteness" refer to real social kinds still with us, despite their fluidity and instability. Hence our use of these terms is not fundamentally a form of false consciousness, despite the many false and mythic ideas about whites as the vanguard of the human race. We need the term whiteness to be able to refer to a unique phenomenon that cannot be captured by ethnic, national, or any other kind of descriptor term.

"Whiteness," therefore, is not analogous to the term "ether" or "phlogiston" in having no real referent. It is the product of history, and its meanings are interactional and contextual, as I argued in Chapter 1. Race has always been a social kind, and, as social conditions change, social kinds mutate. It is possible that in the future the social kind that is whiteness will no longer exist as a meaningful and useful concept, except in reference to the past. But the material embeddedness of whiteness in both resource distribution and forms of subjectivity strongly suggests that it will remain with us for some time to come.

This does not, however, spell political doom. Although I will argue against the eliminativist option, a more accurate and nuanced assessment of what whiteness consists of, and the limits of what it can explain, will reveal that transforming our understanding of whiteness is vital, not simply as a strategic rearticulation, but as a descriptive corrective. The effort of premature erasure, however, is an obstacle to the very transformed understandings we need.

Many antiracist activists and theorists agree that, as a socially constructed "kind," whiteness still makes up a part of our social reality. The left-wing push to abolish whiteness is not based in denying racism or the power of white identity so much as it is motivated by a fatalism about the ability of whiteness to disentangle itself from white supremacy.

However, while pessimism may be in order, fatalism is not. Fatalism presumes an essentialist take on the meanings of white identity, stripping it of its context of use and removing it from the flows of history. What "whiteness" refers to has a political variability in understanding and practice, as variable as white people themselves.

It is crucial to remember that whiteness can refer to multiple things. For example, it can refer to a specified group of human beings associated with particular historical genealogies, or to an idea about white vanguardism, or to a mythic aspect of a nationalist identity, etc. When we use whiteness to refer to ideas or myths, it becomes defined in terms of racism. But when we use it to refer to people, we are using it to give a description of a social group, not a social attitude.

Aryan and Caucasian Myths

Let us look at the genealogy of some racial terms that do seem to be indelibly bound to racist origins. These would include the designation "Aryan," but also, according to Bruce Baum (2006), the designation "Caucasian." Both terms refer to ethno-racial categories with bogus genealogies that have now been decisively disputed by scholars. Although the term "Aryan" is no longer used much except by obstinately bigoted political groups, the term "Caucasian" has changed its usage to become something like a synonym for whiteness, without necessarily being attached to its originating theory that Europeans are the peoples who migrated from the Caucasus.

As Baum's judicial and detailed analysis of the convoluted history of the term Caucasian reveals, it was an invented concept, based on specious grounds and racist intent, traceable to a 1795 work of Hans Blumenbach. Blumenbach, a student of Carl Linnaeus, one of the founders of biological classification systems, developed the taxonomy of racial categorization widely used until the twentieth century that divided human groups into the Caucasian, the Mongolian, the Ethiopian, the American, and the Malay. He chose the term Caucasian to designate what he called the "white" people of Europe because of what he believed to be their geographical origin. But Blumenbach further explained his choice of the term by saying that the Caucasus and its contiguous regions "produces the most beautiful race of men, I mean the Georgian; *and* because all physiological reasons converge to this, that in this region, if anywhere, it seems we ought with the greatest probability to place the authochthones [meaning, indigenous or native] of mankind" (quoted in Baum 2006, 5–6). I italicized the "and" in this statement to highlight Blumenbach's odd conjunction of reasons that includes the beauty of the Georgians as well as his belief that whites were the original humans. Baum concludes from his study of the varied history of the term Caucasian that the concept of race is a political project, or "an effect of power," with no referent in the real world (Baum 2006, 8).

Baum's historical account of the term Caucasian is persuasive, but concepts also experience semantic transformation as their social contexts change. The term Caucasian itself was contested by the Nazis: they refused to believe that all white people were from the Caucasus, preferring the theory that Europe itself produced various white races. Today, I would suggest, the term "Caucasian" is losing its use in liberal societies: it sounds old-fashioned, and appears uncomfortably parallel to the other geographical terms that Blumenbach invented as a way to categorize human difference. He used the term "Mongolian" to designate all peoples from the continent of Asia, with the idea that they all originated from the area of Mongolia. These genealogies have become discredited by more recent archaeological evidence and have mostly dropped out of usage.

The dispute over the term "Aryan" is also instructive. Some scholars argue that, before the Nazis misused the term, it was never a racial term associated with a certain phenotype but a social one designating linguistic origin. In fact, Aryans were not originally white at all, emerging from the region of the world that is today India. If this is right, the term "Aryan" could today be refashioned to refer to an actual group or lineage, without the racist myth. The question is, does either the term Aryan or Caucasian have a significant everyday usage that would justify an effort to correct their fallacious definitions? Or are they of interest mainly for historical purposes, less so for the everyday present? To what might we say, today, that they refer?

Consider this. One can say that the doctrine of National Socialism was irretrievably racist, since in this case we have a set of texts along with historical events that show little variety in regard to matters concerning race and racialism. But historically developing races and ethnicities are not bound in the same way to any set of central texts or originary doxastic commitments. Unlike nations, social groups lack a specifiably distinct textual basis that inhibits their flexibility. The genesis of black identity in concepts of natural slavery did not keep African peoples of the new world from transforming the accepted meanings of blackness. By their linguistic as well as political practice, the term "blackness" lost its nineteenth-century association with natural slavishness or brutishness to eventually gain more positive connotations such as we associate it with today: community solidarity, emotional strength, cultural brilliance, and sophisticated coolness (for a light-hearted and bemused take on these common associations, see

Thurston 2012). The connotations and meanings of blackness have decisively shifted as a result of changing conditions and collective resistance. Nuyorican identity has undergone a similar transformation from its genesis in forced economic migration under colonial conditions. Long derided by both island Puerto Ricans and non-Latinos in the US, Nuyorican identity has become a positive self-ascription signifying survival, political resistance, and cultural and linguistic dexterity (Flores and Yudice 1993). This is not to say that the meanings and political effects of such terms as blackness or Nuyorican are settled or uniform, but that both the content and the valence of common usage have changed so much that self-ascription is generally associated with pride, not resignation or shame.

The genealogy of whiteness – even though it has an origin in domination rather than oppression – is not necessarily determinative of all the future meanings whiteness might develop. Outside the US there are a number of similarly challenged identity concepts that have also been undergoing transformations, from the mestizo identities in Latin America that include the conquistadors alongside the conquered, to German national identity, British identity, and Japanese identity, among others, each wrestling with shameful histories (see e.g. Fulbrook 1999; Morley and Robins 2001).[1] These forms of identity share with whiteness a history of association with supremacist narratives that have now lost credibility. They are in a process of similar turmoil.

---

1 One might be tempted to think that most of these are national, not racial or ethnic, identities. Yet the idea of being "Japanese" or "British" has clear associations with specifically cultural ways of being in the world we associate with ethnicities, with specific cultural histories and practices. The way the concept of "nationality" is understood colloquially, I'd argue, is not entirely distinct from ethnic or ethno-racial concepts. This is why we have trouble imagining Latinos and Asians, in particular, as capable of serving as paradigmatic Americans. For arguments against the easy separability of national, racial, and ethnic identity formations, see Alcoff 2008 and 2010.

Fundamentally, however, political strategies cannot maintain total power over the meaning, and meaningfulness, of terms, except insofar as they can generate a series of events and social structures that bring social phenomena – such as group formations – into existence. Once the group is formed, however, it may develop its own ideas about its identity.

White Labor

Even those whites who come to participate in the coalition for social change, who are active in their local labor union, environmental group, Pride March, Slut Walk, or whatever, come to the group or the event *as whites*, not just as women, gays and lesbians, working-class people, or the disabled, etc. Whiteness is part of what they bring to the equation, for good or bad. They do not show up at such events or meetings only in the guise of one (or more) of their other group-related identities; these intersect with race and ethnicity such that they manifest differently depending on the specific intersections (as well as on their idiosyncratic individual histories, it should go without saying). To say that, "as Joe the Plumber, I come to the union meeting as 'just' a worker" can be an attempt to jumpstart an easy talk of commonality, of brotherhood or sisterhood or class solidarity, allowing Joe to avoid reflecting on the political salience of the differences he may have with others. My argument is not that whiteness overdetermines every encounter, or overpowers every other aspect of one's identity, nor would I hold that whiteness is relevant in every interaction. But it is a danger to believe that whiteness can be left behind.

White identity has substantive features beyond being embroiled in the history of racism, just as oppressed identities are not reducible to their oppression. We need the analytic category of whiteness to be able to mark and name these specifics, *whether or not* the persons so named self-ascribe as whites. As Michael Monahan's study (2011) shows, the 50,000 Irish laborers – men, women and children, who were forcibly transported to Barbados and Virginia in the first half of the seventeenth century to work as indentured servants – had rough lives, and sometimes this led them to make common cause with the forced laborers from Africa (2011, 56; see also O'Callaghan 2000, 9). But to understand the particular position of the Irish indentured workers in the organization of labor in the Caribbean and the Americas, we need the category of whiteness. Despite their racialization as a distinct race from the British, the skin color of the Irish also differentiated them from the African laborers. The Irish subsequently came to have specific opportunities, challenges, and experiences, certainly different from the British colonial settlers, but also different from the Africans, and these latter differences became more important as the practice of race-based inherited enslavement began to spread. The specter of "white slavery" troubled even the British, who warned of a devolving devaluation if Irish labor becomes "as cheap as those of Negroes" (O'Callaghan 2000, 96; quoted in Monahan 2011, 69). The recurring motif of "white slavery" itself indicated a specialized concern not with slavery per se, but with the fate of whites across national and ethnic lines. The period of history Monahan relates predated Blumenbach's designation of the term "Caucasian race" and the common interpellation of whiteness across all European ethnicities, and yet we need the category, or something like it, to understand the specific situation of the Irish. While arguments against enslaving the Irish raised the issue of the domino effects of enslaving white people, arguments against enslaving Africans had to rely on generic humanist claims, since too many for too long thought Africans better off as slaves in the Americas than in their own cultures.[1]

---

1 See, e.g., the views of Robert E. Lee in Korda 2014.

The category of whiteness does not always depend for its analytical utility on self-ascription or explicit use; it is sometimes legitimate to import a concept into a historical period as a way to explain social relations and transformations, as some argue we should do with identity terms such as heterosexual, homosexual, and transgender. The meaning of whiteness can be affected by overt ascriptions, but it is not dependent upon them.

In particular, I want to urge us to let go of the idea that workers ever entered the modern colonial capitalist world system as generic workers, as if their class identity and class interests and class-related opportunities are separable from other elements of their identity. As I argued in Chapter 1, white workers today come to their union bargaining committees with a distinct set of experiences and interests that inform their overall priorities. For example, whites in general may not prioritize the demand for four-week vacations, although this demand is often vital for immigrant workers whose families live long distances away. White workers might prefer more three-day weekends spaced throughout the year so they can take short trips and have days off for other activities, and be content with a two-week vacation once a year. White workers may also not place the same value on in-house transfers, which give those in lower-paid job assignments an advantage when they apply to a job opening in a different department with higher wages. However, in-house transfers can be the only means for some nonwhite workers, hired in as janitors, for example, to advance to more lucrative positions that are usually majority white, such as electrician.

White workers may have valid differences with other groups over how to prioritize the issues for a contract campaign, and the group as a whole will have to negotiate over which unified set of proposals to put to management. Solidarity is obviously vital, so management understands that work stoppages will be supported across different groups of workers. But solidarity is threatened if the priorities of any group of workers are perpetually ignored.

White workers are also likely to come with some baggage of chauvinism and racism, like all other groups, but with the important difference that they are likely to be influenced by the ideology of white vanguardism, the idea that white people are the moral, political, scientific, and technological vanguard of the human race. This is a powerful cross-class phenomenon, conferring a sense of dignity and entitlement on men, and women, of modest means. Yet in the context of a shared political and economic project, white workers can change longstanding assumptions and behavioral patterns.

The proof of this is a changed set of priorities and practices in many parts of the US labor movement itself. The change from craft unions to industrial unions played an important role in shifting away from strategies focused almost exclusively on protecting the value accorded certain skilled jobs that were usually dominated by white males to strategies designed for a diversity of job assignments and skill levels. Subsequent organizing had to develop new forms. Because of the typically racial and gendered segmentation of job assignments, often workers are separated, physically and socially, in their work sites. Even when departments are more diverse, however, workers come to the job from different neighborhoods and schools. Effective unions strive to create opportunities for community building in which new experiences can emerge across these silos of difference. This can occur at parties and picnics but also in ongoing committee work and, most intensely, during periods of strikes.

Several unions and union locals have largely repudiated gender-, sexuality-, and race-based chauvinisms, ended US protectionist policies, trained shop stewards on issues for transgender workers, and developed smartly crafted practices to avoid segregating the workforce based on those who have documentation and those who do not (such as rendering such differences null in the way contracts are written). There has been a sea change in the recent US labor movement compared with a previous era when major unions made alliances with the CIA in Central America, upheld Jim Crow in their constitutions, and neglected organizing in female sectors of the workforce. Race and gender divisions crippled the movement, allowing advances in only small craft sectors that were easily weakened by outsourcing, subcontracting, and hiring scabs from the masses of underemployed people of color. Today's unions cannot afford to repeat these mistakes, and they now organize among diverse sectors of the economy, such as healthcare workers, teachers, and janitors, while recruiting heavily from communities of color for staff positions. They practice affirmative action in their hiring and in representations at national conventions. The movement as a whole is in the process of learning a new skill set needed for leading a diverse workforce into successful struggle against a more mobile transnational capital. What is required is not simply overturning the exclusionary practices and attitudes of the past, but productively negotiating ongoing differences among the workforce.

There are still major hurdles to cross, without question. As the experienced labor leaders Bill Fletcher and Fernando Gapasin (2008) put it "the United States has never had a true labor movement, only a segmented struggle of workers." They urge unions to reject easy claims that "we're all one working class" (2008, 237). Through detailed case studies of numerous campaigns, Fletcher and Gapasin argue that "twenty-first-century unionism cannot view class oppression simply as an economic concept that exists in isolation from other forms of oppression in capitalist society" (2008, 168). In practice, this means engaging in struggles beyond the workplace, understanding that class struggle also involves fights around gentrification, the distributions of toxic waste, and educational inequality. Falsely invoking commonalities among workers will only hinder the effort to create a true *labor* movement rather than one that represents a segregated portion of the labor force.

Three Arguments Against Eliminativism

Despite the objective social realities of white identity, and the importance of acknowledging it in social justice movements, many have been seduced by the idea that whiteness can be left behind. Cosmopolitanists like Kwame Anthony Appiah (2005) and Jason Hill (2000) and critics of identity politics such as Jodi Dean (1996) would have us downplay social identities in the political realm, while race traitor advocates like Noel Ignatiev and John Garvey (1996) argue that whiteness is constituted through and through by racism, that racism is its founding moment, and will be its dying gasp.

I have three basic arguments against the eliminativists. Two of these have already been alluded to; a third will be advanced anew.

First, eliminativists have a wrong account of what social identities are. In particular, there is often a set of mistaken assumptions about whiteness as merely an ideology inflicted from the state that obscures and misdirects more than it explains and is basically a kind of collective illusion. In Chapter 1, I offered four desiderata of social identities in general, and three ways to approach whiteness in particular. Here I will elaborate on the ways that this account pushes against the eliminativist project.

1 Social identities are not created entirely from the top down. Omi and Winant's (1994) theory of racial formation provides a realistic account of historical processes wherein *multiple* actors influence events from *varied* social locations. Racial concepts are products of both resistance movements and oppressive forces, and, as such, whiteness cannot be blamed exclusively on state and corporate actors. Rather, its meaning has also become congealed around a set of retrograde political tendencies displayed by white people at all levels of society. Importantly, however, this means that future

alterations in white subjectivity and practice can alter what it means to be white.

2 Social identities are rough indices of the relationship between individuals and macro historical events, such as slavery, genocide, land annexation, famines, religious persecution, and imperial wars. These indices have explanatory value for both individual lives and historical events. Groups are positioned differently in regard to such histories, as subject to violence or as benefiting from the spoils of war. Such collective differences can partially determine affective responses for generations in the form of selective empathy for certain veterans over others or rage at new events that trigger reminders of the oppression of one's forebears. Given these group-related responses, we can use a category like whiteness to name a broad and diverse collective experience with the capacity to explain phenomena today, from wealth differentials, to political dispositions, to affective patterns.

3 Social identities are also correlated to unconscious practices, modes of comportment, and habits of perception, as the social psychology literature has established. But I'd suggest that these empirical studies simply confirm a generally accepted truth: that different people interact, think, and perceive differently in sometimes group-related ways. Sonia Sotomayor's (2002) controversial claim that a "wise Latina" would judge differently simply names the commonly held belief that identities can sometimes affect our judgments and interpretations (Alcoff 2010).

4 Finally, social identities need to be understood as aspects of our shared material world in the sense that they are (generally) visible features that produce a kind of visual registry directing us toward specific forms of interaction. Identities are not merely a discursive overlay on top of materially instantiated differences, in which case it might indeed seem that we could simply, and volitionally, change the discourse and thus change the society.

Rather than being simply "in our heads," identities are part of our social worlds. Changing the meanings and significance of social identities will require changing the material conditions of our society.

These four elements show social identities to be real material aspects of social worlds rather than mythic overlays that can be discursively corrected.

My second argument against eliminativism is that the history of those people marked as white indicates a specific experience as well as some level of consciousness about their different social situation and options. In other words, whiteness is not just an ideological formulation. As Linebaugh and Rediker's (2000) work on the multiracial mariner working class shows, the material reality of racial formations has a long and politically complex history, and in some cases we need to read whiteness *back* into history to explain the different trajectory of groups.

To speak meaningfully of whites, however, requires further specifications of the domain, because "white experience," or "white history," is just too broad and internally diverse to have any content. But a suitably contextualized or hyphenated whiteness is an aspect of people's experiences, for example, coming to the new world as Irish economic refugees, or French farmers, or German shopkeepers. The integration of whites across national and ethnic distinctions, and their treatment *as whites*, led to the formation of expressive cultural forms, such as clogging, detective fiction, and what we today call country music. The fact that none of these forms emerged without being profoundly influenced by the cultures of other groups simply means that white cultures share the same hybrid, multiply informed genealogy as all other cultures; the only difference was that white racists claimed that whiteness was the "uncaused cause," or pure self-invention with no external influence. However, while this purely "white history" was largely a myth, it remains the case that there is a historical experience of diverse groups of whites for whom the fact of their interpellation as whites played a role in the practices and customs they developed.

Monica McDermott's (2006) excellent ethnography of working-class whites and Dana Ste. Claire's (1998) history of the folklore of "Florida Crackers" are just two recent examples of the sorts of studies emerging that reveal the fluid formations of present day white identities. McDermott illustrates the experiences and subjectivity of contemporary working-class whites who work in corner stores. Her project is not to show how the historical essence of white identity continues to manifest privileges up to the present, as in an uninterrupted continuation of the same, but rather, how white identity is lived in a real-world context. Through a method of participant ethnography in two distinct urban settings, Boston and Atlanta, McDermott finds that "whiteness does not function in an unambiguous fashion. In racially mixed working-class and poor areas, whiteness can serve as a hindrance as well as a mark of privilege" (2006, 38). Moreover, many whites take their poverty to indicate their own weakness or failure precisely because, even as whites, they cannot escape poor neighborhoods. Yet another finding of her study is that antiblack prejudice can persist among white Americans in a way that coexists with "friendliness, civility, and an avowed opposition to explicit racial discrimination" (2006, ix).

In a study described as part anthropology, part history, and part folklore, Ste. Claire describes early twentieth-century rural white Floridians, the subjects, and agents, of what was positively avowed as "cracker culture." These were poor whites such as my own forebears, eking out an agricultural-based living under harsh tropical environments with little existing infrastructure in place. The term cracker in this context referred to Florida-born whites living in the backcountry who had developed an impressive know-how in dealing with alligators, venomous snakes, mosquitoes, and sandy soil. For them, the term cracker is still used today with a certain amount of pride, signifying self-sufficiency and the honesty of "plain folk."

Works such as those by McDermott and Ste. Claire give a content to white identities beyond either the supremacist myths or the manipulations of elite institutions, which included, of course, until recently, most academic research. Despite the specificity that such ethnographies reveal, there is no plausible case to be made that whiteness is not a central aspect of these collective identity formations.

Yet eliminativism may be intended more as a prescription for the future than as a description of either the present or the past. My third argument addresses this prescriptive project.

The quest, or desire, to eliminate whiteness in the future may in fact be motivated by a desire to escape from uncomfortable histories that bear on present day material distributions, or the simple desire to transcend historical guilt. Let's consider this idea, for a moment, in the context of the award-winning film, *Avatar* (2009). *Avatar*, as has often been stated, is a version of *Dances with Wolves* set in space – the latter won the Academy Award for Best Picture in 1991. The two movies have a strikingly similar plot, both centered on conversion experiences of white men who discover they are on the wrong side, but beyond this there are revealing political differences. In *Dances with Wolves*, Lieutenant John Dunbar of the Union Army stationed on the Indian frontier gets to know some members of the nearby Lakota tribe, and through this begins to realize that he is fighting on the wrong side of the Indian Wars. He quickly learns the high price of treason to the white power structure, but by the end of the movie he nevertheless commits to return to white society and attempt to spread his new knowledge. Before coming to this decision, he considers the possibility of attempting to assimilate to Lakota society, and he pairs off with a Lakota/white woman, Stands with a Fist, who assimilated as a child. But he realizes that the more responsible action would be for them both to try to change white views about the Indians.

Thus Dunbar, who was named "Dances with Wolves" by the Lakota, rides off in the sunset to a difficult and uncertain future. His aim is not to provide ethnographies of native life for white people, but, in a sense, to provide critical ethnographies of whites for whites, thus thwarting the continuation of white vanguardism.

Now let's jump ahead nearly 20 years to *Avatar*, a movie whose magnum profits indicate that its narrative resonates with broad numbers of the white public. Its not just the 3-D visuals that drew viewers, but the Star Wars-like story, which pits a plucky group of underdog anti-imperialists in space against a death star of corporate bad guys.

The main protagonist is again a white guy who becomes a traitor to his people. This time, the story is set in the future and not the past (though both movies take us comfortably out of the present). Jake Sully is a seriously disabled Marine veteran recruited to a new mission at an outpost where an indigenous people, the N'avi, are blocking an aggressive quest for resources. This time the evil community is multiracial, making it a more realistic representation of the future. And while it is no longer completely male-dominated, there is no indication that this society set in the future has achieved real racial or gender equality; the principal leaders are white and male and they act with impunity, despite opposition from white women and people of color.

Sully is able to achieve a kind of literal double consciousness through a science fiction device of avatar existence, in which he escapes the limits of his paraplegic body to experience life as an able-bodied N'avi, or at least as himself in N'avi form. As he moves back and forth between his white and his new blue identity, Sully seems at first to retain a white subjectivity with only a change of bodily form, but by the end it has become clear that he wants to shed his white identity entirely, and to become "one of them."

The interstellar imperialists from Earth whom Sully works for are referred to as Sky People by the N'avi. As an avatar, Sully must learn to navigate between two sets of names and titles and terms, as well as two ways of interacting with others and of inhabiting a planet. Watching Sully navigate his bipolar world must, I would suggest, resonate with whites sitting in the audience who are beginning to realize that theirs is *not* the only language, philosophy, morality, or aesthetics around, and may not be the best in all respects even if it has the superficial superiority of instrumental domination over an environment.

Importantly, the white male protagonist in *Avatar*, just as in *Dances With Wolves*, must accept being a novice student in terms of the nonwhite culture. Sully is teased and called both a baby and a moron while he is trying to learn N'avi ways. But he not only has to learn everything from scratch; he also has to unlearn everything he already knows. There is a telling moment when the elder female leader of the N'avi expresses some skepticism about changing the Sky People's thinking, asking, "how can we fill a thing that is already filled up?" She is asking, in other words, how the Sky People can be taught about the N'avi when they think they already know all there is to be known? Indeed, the movie plays out a constant epistemic contestation between knowledge systems as well as ways of knowing or modes of justification, between the N'avi's spiritual metaphysics of nature and the Sky People's instrumental rationality and environmental atheism.[1] Here then is presented in dramatic form the obstacle to transformation: how can whiteness revise itself when this requires not merely learning new things, but a fundamental *unlearning* that will change all it believes about *itself*?

---

1 *Avatar* stereotypes both dominant and oppressed cultures, portraying the former as irredeemably violent as well as willfully and dogmatically ignorant, and the latter as naturally peaceful and communal. There is a little more complexity in *Dances with Wolves*, although this is achieved by portraying native peoples as coming in two simplistic archetypes: civilized and peaceful, like the Lakota, and bloodthirsty and uncivilized, like the Pawnee. For a more critical take on *Dances with Wolves*, see Sirota 2013; for balanced views, see Bird 1996.

Sully, as a non-elite member of the lower ranks of a colonizing power, becomes representative of the white everyman. He's been forced into his current high-risk job as an avatar because, lacking access to healthcare, he was promised a transplant if he performs well. Interestingly, there is a similar element in *Dances with Wolves*, since it was Dunbar's impending disability – his fear that he would lose his injured leg in the overtaxed army hospitals of the Civil War – that propelled him to the suicidal ride that classified him (mistakenly) as a hero and thus able to escape to the western frontier. The filmmakers evidently assume that audiences will identify with protagonists motivated by the desire to escape disability even at the risk of death. But this narrative device also means that the white hero is, in both cases, someone who comes to learn the false claims of white male invincibility, as well as the idea that white-dominant society can always be relied upon to take care of its own. Dunbar knows that the indifferent, overworked army medics will simply cut off his leg, and Sully knows that the indifferent military corporation could easily fund his cure, but will only do so, like any good Mafia Don, after he performs a dangerous and unsavory service. The limited reach of white patronage surely plays a role in spurring their conversions.

Despite their similarities, *Avatar* ends in a significantly different way from *Dances with Wolves*. Unlike Dunbar, Sully loses his whiteness at the close of the movie and becomes fully assimilated to the N'avi, both physically and culturally, refusing to return to his own people. The imperialist culture of the Sky People is portrayed as so monomaniacal that the idea of a revolution is hopeless. It is notable that in less than 20 years, we might read the collective white unconscious as becoming more pessimistic, rather than less, about the possibility of changing white cultures. However, in *Avatar*, even if it cannot be changed, the white culture can be beaten, at least in a specific battle site. In a burst of implausible physical prowess and military leadership, Sully beats back the imperial army to become the greatest warrior the N'avi have ever known. This too marks a significant difference from *Dances with Wolves*, where Dunbar's capacity as a warrior is never presented as superior to the Lakota. The difference in ending is significant. In *Avatar*, even though Sully ostensibly assimilates and literally turns blue, he maintains a position of dominance – as the smartest and the bravest and the recognized military leader. The white audience has the reassuring experience of seeing the white man move from dunce to leader in the time it takes to watch a movie. And he also wins the love of the chief's beautiful daughter, despite her prior betrothal to another N'avi.

If we read *Avatar*, then, as an expression of at least one important trend within collective white consciousness, we can see that it is still within the same broad historical moment as *Dances with Wolves*, a moment characterized by the disaffection with white vanguard narratives. But we can also read in *Avatar* a regressive development from *Dances with Wolves*. Sully does not take the difficult path of returning to the white world to enact social change from within. Instead, at the end we see him enjoying the benefits of the nonwhite communal culture. He loses his white identity in the sense of physical form, but also as a specific and substantive way of life, yet this loss is portrayed, interestingly, as holding nothing of value. *Avatar* provides white audiences who are uncomfortably conscious of the false claims of white vanguardism with a way out of this discomfort that requires no sacrifice. The movie titles themselves signal this regression, from one that conveys the indigenous point of view – the Lakota name for Dunbar – to one that signifies a mobile transformer, the very activity of which is associated not with the heavily tradition bound nonwhite ethnic cultures, but with the mercurial capacity of western capital, and western man, to go anywhere and become anything.

Such a contradictory outcome – losing one's whiteness, but retaining white dominance – is clearly not what the race traitor, white abolitionists, or even the cosmopolitans have in mind. And yet, Sully's repudiation of white-dominant culture and his rejection of his own white identity are as dramatic and complete as any eliminativist could want. Thus I want to suggest here a concordance between the eliminativist's quest to escape whiteness and the avatar's beatific assimilation as being symptomatic of the current turmoil of whiteness. Having a white identity has become a heavy burden to bear, with its indelible connection to a disquieting past, troubling present, and correlate responsibilities. The regressive quest is how to maintain a pride in one's identity and one's forebears without sacrificing, à la Tea Party, one's rational faculties.

To summarize these three arguments against eliminativism, I have made the case that whiteness is not simply a form of linguistic misdirection orchestrated by elites, but an organic aspect of our current social ontology, and that the quest for escape is symptomatic of the inner turmoil whites feel who have seen through the myths of vanguardism. It is not, however, a politically productive move.

White Double Consciousness

Contemporary white anxiety is manifestly in a quest for a resolution to its troubled form of double consciousness, but this can take both regressive and progressive forms. The regressive versions aim for a comforting escape hatch, while the truly progressive version seeks a morally responsible way to acknowledge and learn from the horrific history of white vanguardism without foreclosing the possibility of playing a role in future positive change. *Avatar* symbolizes the regressive version with near perfection.

Although I have placed this quest in a contemporary frame of reference, connecting it to post-Vietnam US culture and current anxieties about the impending demographic shifts, there were many earlier manifestations of unease over the claims of global white supremacy. The best-selling British novelist Graham Greene began linking US imperialism to racism in the 1950s in a series of novels with a wide American readership. The most famous of these, *The Quiet American*, was adapted twice on screen with quintessential American actors playing the problematic lead: first Audie Murphy, and, more recently, Brendan Fraser. In a less mainstream sector of society, various communist and socialist groups in the US began to grapple seriously with issues of whiteness from the 1930s on, and sectarian differences between parties often centered precisely on issues of nationalism and degrees of support for anticolonial movements (Elbaum 2002). The Beats provided the most famous attempt to escape from whiteness through a self-presentation of sensibilities that they characterized as nonwhite. They presented themselves as having non-normative modes of being, not simply as adopting nonwhite styles of cultural expression, music, and writing. The novelist Jack Kerouac, in particular, expressed a poignant alienation from his white identity and the general normative whiteness of heterosexual suburbia, and he emphatically identified with the more intense existential registers of nonwhite affect that he took to be common among African Americans and Mexicans.[1]

Although Kerouac is humorously oblivious to the racist way he characterizes African Americans and Mexicans, I would suggest that we should take his alienated consciousness seriously as a phenomenological datum from which to understand the transformations of whiteness. That is, we should take seriously his experience of alienation from the normative cultural and political meanings that a white appearance would convey in the 1950s, and how this manifested as discomfort with his embodied identity. It's useful to consider Kerouac's alienated consciousness in relation to Du Bois's notion of double consciousness as "two souls, two thoughts" inhabiting a single

---

1 I discuss Kerouac's identity issues at greater length in *Visible Identities* (2006), ch. 11.

body, invoking the idea of seeing oneself by conflicting meaning-systems, inside and outside of one's community. The contradictions between these points of reference can produce a troubled, hyper-aware consciousness. Kerouac's troubles had a different source from those of minoritized groups, yet they had similar effects. He knew how normative middle-class whites viewed the world; he also knew how partial this view was and he had an inkling (though just an inkling) of another possibility. Thus he experienced a kind of split self, unable to immerse fully into normative whiteness, yet still haunted by its expectations.

Du Bois's concept of African Americans' double consciousness is thus resonant with the incoherence of white subjective experience, but with important differences. For Du Bois, the two perspectives of double consciousness are contradictory, impossible to render into a coherent view: he calls it "two warring ideals in one dark body, whose dogged strength alone keeps it from being torn asunder" (1997/1903, 38). Importantly, though, the way in which black people are seen by whites is almost wholly false, so the potential relativism of the epistemic conflict is muted. The same incoherence can also beset whites who are taken as the vanguard of the human race while knowing they are not, yet the main source for white enlightenment often comes not from a supportive and resistant community of brethren, but from outsiders. Like Beauvoir, whites may come to realize the social meanings of whiteness, its unearned privileges and moral collusion, once they begin to intuit how they are viewed by nonwhite others. This is a critical difference. Whites who experience a split consciousness between the way they see themselves and the way they are seen by nonwhite others are not thereby oppressed by a racist gaze from racial *others*. Rather, they are living out the necessary effects of white vanguardist ideologies. Their new-found incoherence is a potential source for a new and more accurate understanding of social conditions. Coming to this means becoming aware of the obstacles in the way of creating a morally livable white identity, an identity that is both white and morally defensible. This is an obstacle that can be approached in a number of different ways, from denial to political activism.

I want to suggest that the current subjectivity of many whites today does not correspond to the dominant narrative of whiteness that holds itself ahead of and better than every other culture. In some cases, their own experience of their work lives may cohere little with supremacist claims. So beyond Kerouac's cultural alienation from the aesthetic norms and values of his upper-middle-class family, there can also be an alienation felt by poor whites, rural whites, or less educated whites, whites who work as waitresses and as sanitation workers and as schoolroom cafeteria workers, or whites who come as new immigrants from eastern Europe to fill low-wage jobs. For these whites, the notion of privilege and the promised entitlements to the vanguard feel pretty meaningless. There are also those whites whose multiracial families, neighborhoods, and workplaces are changing their affective lives as well as their perceptual practices and habits of action. This is not just (or necessarily) a doxastic repudiation of the tenets of white supremacy, or a change at the level of belief, but, more importantly, an alteration of lived context and resultant consciousness and modes of behavior.

In some cases, the turmoil in white subjectivity and embodied existence, and the incoherence of an alienated consciousness, produces a genuine disaffection from white supremacy, even if occurring in confused, inchoate form. But there is without a doubt a growing awareness about how whites are viewed by others as well as a significant decrease in white cultural domination and segregated social life. In saying that "being white these days is not what it used to be," Nell Painter (2012, 389) points to the following four trend-lines as important markers of contemporary change. I would note here that these are trends and not, alas, consolidated achievements with universal scope, but they are significant nonetheless.

(1) *Whiteness is neither as normative nor as positive an identity as it used to be.* This is simply to say that it is no longer so easy to see whites as the singular norm or default position (Painter 2012, 388). Critical race and whiteness studies have helped bring this about in the academy, but ethnographic research shows young whites beyond the campuses acutely self-conscious about their whiteness and decidedly uncomfortable with its associated meanings (see, e.g., Gallagher 1994; Allen 2004; Richeson and Trawalter 2008). Although they express a disinclination to think about their whiteness, avoidance of nonwhite perspectives and cultural expressions is almost impossible. Whites thus find themselves the object of a new gaze that foregrounds their whiteness in ways that are not always flattering.

(2) *The degree to which white identity alone confers privilege is mediated more so than in the past by the significance of other variables – class, gender, region, age, able-bodiedness, sexuality, and so on.* According to economist Richard Wolff (2009), the real wages of white workers rose steadily over a century until the 1970s, from which time there has been a steady drop. The increasing gap between rich and poor has thrown millions of whites into economic instability, and the new feudal relations of production have shown evidence of a clear-cut disregard for the well-being of white workers in industrialized nations. The attack on the wages and benefits of millions of unionized public sector workers has mobilized white workers from Wisconsin to Maine. And the loss of well-paid manufacturing jobs – from steel to auto to textile – and the forced march to the service sector have notably hit white male workers, who made up the bulk of that sector of the workforce. A recent study by Michael Zweig, Michael Porter, and Yuxiang Huang (2011) shows that the instances of US casualties in Afghanistan are disproportionately white, very different from the deaths in Vietnam which were disproportionately

black and Latino. Thus, Painter may be right that the terms of the old racial contract have shifted. This is not about white victimization: whites are not targeted because they are white in the way nonwhite racial and ethnic groups are targeted, but their whiteness provides little defense against the economic contractions of imperial capitalism (Wolff 2009).

(3) *White expectations of being able to have a white-dominant or white-only home or personal space are decreasing.* White-dominant neighborhoods and schools are becoming less white, and the media that constantly invades every moment of our personal space is less white as well. Whites remain less likely than any other racial group in the US to marry outside their race, and yet the numbers of white exogamous unions are steadily rising so that, by 2050, it is projected that 10 percent of whites will marry people from other races. This phenomenon can coexist with racism, as Obama's family, Bush's family, and my own can attest, and yet the *younger* generations that grow up in such families may be less "filled up" with the old ideas of their parents and grandparents, ideas that seem to survive for the older generation despite experiential changes wrought by having mixed race families. Hence the children who grow up in such mixed families may learn new ways of being in the world by seeing through multiple lenses.

(4) *The promulgation of new racial categories may confuse the meaning of the concept of race and lessen its power.* There are certainly many confused and confusing new categories of race: in the 2010 Census, the ability to check more than one box means that a full 63 racial types are now recognized. The singular significance of race, Painter suggests, loses its punch when it gets diluted to this degree (2012, 385). We cannot forget that the promulgation of mixed race categories can easily coexist with white dominance and antiblack and/or anti-indigenous racisms, as it does in Latin

America. Nonetheless, Painter is hopeful that the current trend is less an expansion of types than a muddying of distinctions that will render racism's directive more obscure. What will eventually develop in the United States will undoubtedly reflect the particular history, mix of groups, and forms of resistance *here*, rather than being determined merely to repeat and replay dynamics elsewhere.

These trends represent the objective foundation for the turmoil in white subjectivity. The experiences of whites are changing not because the society they live in is multiracial, since this has always been the case, but because their society is more racially integrated in its cultural and political identity, a trend that will expand with demographic changes. And the meaning of both whiteness and of white privilege will undoubtedly change as race categories are multiplied and increasingly diversified within. Charting these trends against the turmoil already manifest in white consciousness should help us, I would hope, to avoid being deterministic about the future.

Part of this white turmoil is, however, as we all know, pure reaction. Within two years after the election of Barack Obama, the number of hate groups nationwide increased to more than 900. Anti-government, or so-called patriot, groups tripled, to 1,200. And nativist extremist groups of the kind that harass immigrants – engaging in what they call "beaner hunting" – saw the largest increase, 80 percent, to a total of 1,600. Don't assume you know where all of these groups are: while there are 32 hate groups in Alabama, there are 31 in New York State, 44 in New Jersey, and 60 in California. And don't assume these groups are harmless. The month that Obama was elected, in November 2008, gun sales reached a record high of 1.5 million.[1]

---

1 These and other related facts can be found at the Southern Poverty Law Center website: http://www.splcenter.org. The gun sales statistics are from the FBI.

We might easily, and plausibly, blame the inflammatory media for spreading disinformation and directing the action just as effectively as I remember Cuban-owned radio stations in Miami used to direct their audiences to show up with bats whenever we organized anti-imperialist marches in the 1970s. But the message of Fox News is working today because it connects to an already felt turmoil. And the white reaction that has emerged in the Tea Party is not made up of the rich or the educated but, according to recent Harris and Quinnipiac polls, decidedly non-elites. Rational, economic-based motivations are simply insufficient to explain the psychic attachment many whites feel to white vanguardism.

Yet the current turmoil in white subjectivity provides a new opportunity to revise the narrative of whiteness. Such a revision must address the motivational question – the question of what motivates whites as whites to reject white supremacy – without reducing this to material gain. If eliminativism is a pipe dream, we must explore the basis upon which whites might join a coalition for social change for their own reasons.

What might those reasons be? Antiracism is, on the face of it, a negative agenda directed at repudiating and overcoming racism and its long legacy. But we also need a positive agenda for changing society. To be involved in such change, whites must come to reassess the meaning of whiteness. Imagining the motivations whites may have for being involved in such a movement consists of at least three strong elements:

1 Whites have a motivation to face the full-on truth of history, to avoid being continuously duped by pampering (white) nationalist narratives. This requires displacing the narratives of vanguardism with new narratives that get the actual histories of the US and Europe in clearer focus, including both the atrocities of colonialism and the actual variety of white experience under white racist regimes. Such narratives would make sense

of the present economic difficulties and cultural contestations in a way that vanguardist narratives cannot, and will suggest new ways to make alliance and coalition. History is a weapon.[1]

2 Social progress by any measure cannot be advanced or achieved by white people alone, given their decreasing numbers and increasing disunity. Whites who support even the milquetoast social reforms offered by the Democratic Party must find allies. Progressive unions have realized this for some time and have initiated a number of new policies to better represent the multiracial working class, as I've discussed. But coalitions are now a necessity for whites of nearly all political persuasions, just as has long been true for other groups. Effective coalitions require facing differences, not turning away from them or attempting to erase them in some reductive dream of a unified discourse.

3 Whites have a motivation to live in communities where they can hold up their heads, and smile without self-consciousness at their neighbors' children. Vanguardism worked in part because it gave whites a positive, moral role in the world. Whites wanted to believe they were providing charity rather than benefiting from the conditions that produced the need for charity; that they defended civility in a barbarous world rather than exacerbating barbarism. The rise of the Christian right is due in part to the power of these motivations to live a moral life. The left needs to learn this lesson.

What would it mean for whites to become more positively embodied as white within a multipolar social landscape? Perhaps the critical element will involve coming to understand whiteness as a mere particular among other particulars, rather than the universal that stands as the exemplar of civilization. The Mexican philosopher Leopoldo Zea explained that, while every culture tends to

---

1 See historyisaweapon.com.

see itself at the center of the world, it was the West that uniquely created a worldview in which it regarded itself "as universal," in which its own history is "world history" (1992, 75–6). What whites do advances the species; what others do reflects only on themselves. Against such a worldview, living whiteness mindfully as a particular would have a deflationary effect, and produce an opening to the possibility of learning more than leading. It would also place whiteness within a complex multipolar history involving varied relations with others, some of which became constitutive of whiteness itself.

A documentary, made in 2006 and directed by James Moll, entitled aptly *Inheritance*, charts the effects of Nazism on German, non-Jewish children. Moll focused on Monika Hertwig, the real-life daughter of the brutal concentration camp commander Amon Goeth, memorably portrayed by Ralph Fiennes in *Schindler's List* (1993) as the sort of sadist who enjoyed shooting prisoners while lounging on his back terrace. Hertwig shares her story of slowly uncovering the facts about her parents with quiet integrity. She eventually reaches out to one of the victims, Helen Jonas, who worked as a servant in the Goeth household and knew Hertwig's father personally. With some trepidation, Hertwig asks to meet with Jonas. Sadness overcomes her as she is faced with the depth of her parent's willful brutality, yet her relationship to a grandchild seems to clarify her decision. We cannot change the past, as she explains, we can only, possibly, change the future.

Conclusion: A Place in the Rainbow

> Slavery is a moral and political evil...[but] it is a greater evil to the white man than to the black race...The blacks are immeasurably better off here than in Africa, morally, socially, and physically. The painful discipline they are undergoing is necessary for their instruction as a race.
>
> General Robert E. Lee, letter to his wife Mary
> (in Korda 2014)

Those lines were penned more than 150 years ago. We may imagine such views today as the provenance of only the extreme and the ignorant, such as the Nevada cattle rancher Cliven Bundy who enjoyed brief fame as a populist everyman until his Lee-like defense of slavery got picked up on a mike that went viral in the Spring of 2014. But this kind of view is actually a cornerstone of US national identity, which views African Americans and other non-white minorities as all hailing from societies that were and remain culturally and politically behind Europe. Hence, their experiences in the United States, however awful, are still better than what their fate would be in their home countries even today. In short, the United States of America is the best of all possible worlds, and no matter how one's family came here, they should be grateful they did.

Washington and Lee University, Virginia, is one of the oldest and most elite institutions of higher education in the South. Founded before the revolutionary war in 1749 as Augusta Academy, its name evolved over the years to mark two crucial benefactors: George Washington, *the* George Washington, who led the revolutionary troops against the British to victory, and Robert E. Lee, General of the Confederate States of America, who led the southern troops in their battle for independence. The name of the university, then, signifies the most radical sort of split one can imagine: the man often credited as the founder of the nation juxtaposed with the general who attempted, less than a century later, to sever the nation in two.

Washington and Lee's publicity materials explain the name as paying homage to the two men who are said to have saved the university's existence. President Washington saved the Academy from financial ruin with a gift of $20,000 in 1796. General Lee is said to have saved it from obscurity when he agreed to a term as president in 1865, serving it until his death in 1870. Lee expanded the school and its programs, although it is still a small and very elite institution. Today it enrolls 2,200 students with a curriculum focused on the liberal arts. It boasts of being the Ivy League of the South, and certainly its costs are comparable to the Ivies: tuition, fees, room and board run about $55,000 per year.

The university's campus is housed beautifully in the small town of Lexington, Virginia, a good 50 minutes from Roanoke, the nearest small city. Lexington has designated as historic landmarks several buildings on the campus as well as in the town that bear Lee's name, such as the Lee Chapel and the Robert E. Lee Building, ensuring that they cannot be torn down, or burned down. Meandering around the campus, as I did recently, one can see everywhere the typical, broad white columns of southern architecture. The confederacy imagined itself to be heir to the colonnaded halls of ancient Greece, another slave society that is routinely named a democracy in our children's textbooks.

The most celebrated historical landmark of the Washington and Lee University campus, and of the town, is the final resting place of Robert E. Lee. He and his family are buried in a mausoleum that sits directly beneath the main campus chapel. It is in this structure, known as the Lee Chapel, that students engage in daily worship and where many of the main campus events are held, from Phi Beta Kappa convocations to faculty meetings to symposia with visiting speakers. Also housed in the basement level of the Lee Chapel is the extensive Lee Museum, which displays historic memorabilia as well as a narrative explanation of Lee's life with a focus on his term as president of the university and his enduring legacy for the institution. The most important feature of that legacy is said to be the model of integrity he sought to instill in all students through the strict Washington and Lee Honor System still in place, which punishes violations with permanent dismissal. Some no doubt view this as an example of the celebrated genteel southern culture that survived the brutality of northern aggression.

Directly upstairs from the museum and the Lee family crypt, the Lee Chapel looks to be a typically ecumenical space with plainly decorated pews. There is a stage and, behind the stage, an altar-like space in which Lee reclines in a recumbent white marble sculpture. Upon first glance, a visitor might mistake this to be the ensculpted remains of the general, as if he is lying in state, but on closer inspection, one can see he appears to be taking a nap. Lee's actual remains are buried just one floor directly below this sculpture. In the corners of this altar space around the sculpture are arrayed exact replicas of several confederate war flags painted with the names of central battle sites. All of this is visible when one sits in the chapel.

Outside the chapel is buried Lee's beloved horse, Traveller, famous for carrying the general through the duration of the war. There is a marker on Traveller's grave, and on the marker sit several pennies. When I asked my host for an explanation of the pennies, she directed me to notice how each was positioned face down. Visitors like to do this, she explained, so that Lincoln's face might be said to be kissing Traveller's ass. Others come along and turn the pennies over in a small show of protest, as I immediately did. Within seconds, another museum guest behind me turned them all over again.

Every January 19, the small town of Lexington is flooded by tourists. This is Robert E. Lee's birthday; it is also Martin Luther King's birthday. So it is that, every year, on the national US holiday for Martin Luther King Day, members of the Sons of the Confederacy hold parades in Lexington, congregate at the location of Lee's grave and drape the town in confederate flags. In years past they were allowed to hang confederate flags from town flagpoles, but finding this indecorous the town council passed an ordinance decreeing that only state and national flags could be flown from town property. The Sons of the Confederacy are still furious about this ruling and have recently hired aerial advertising planes to buzz over the town dragging banners that say "Shame on Lexington." It can feel a little threatening, as one local townsperson related.

There is more than a little tension between some of Lexington's residents and its pro-confederacy tourists, but the Lee Chapel and the Lee Museum seem to have been crafted exactly as the Sons of the Confederacy would have done if they had had unimpeded control over both the design and the contents. There is not a whisper of criticism against the man, hardly a mention of slavery or the fact that he owned slaves, and certainly no extended discussion of how slaves lived in Lexington or what their fate was before, during, or after the war. There is prominent mention of the fact that, before he became general of the confederate army, Lee was asked to head the Union Army, but his choice to lead the confederates is explained, without commentary or interrogation, by his own statement that, as a southerner, he felt a duty to lead the southern troops. It is this sense of duty, via Lee's interpretation of it, that is used to present him as a man of honor and integrity whose life example can continue to instill in students a model of virtuous conduct. In the shop that accompanies the Lee Museum, there is a trove of confederate memorabilia and knick-knacks, from the dishes he used to numerous drawings, sculptures, and paintings made of him during his life. There are tchotchkes such as rulers that carry the names of southern generals and toys such as plush versions of Traveller. There are dozens of books; none is about slavery. As the historian Edward Ball, himself a descendant of rich slaveowners, has put it, "In popular memory – in white memory – the plantations of the antebellum South were like a necklace of country clubs strewn across the land. In reality they were a chain of work camps in which four million were imprisoned" (2015). Ball goes on to make connections between the slave patrols of that era and the racial dragnets of today in which black and brown people face heavily armed police.

The affective response one can have to a place like Washington and Lee University is as intense as it is divergent. I spent two days there speaking on the topic of whiteness. By the last session with students, my temper was close to the surface. I had been housed in the "Lee Room" of the historic Morris House, a museum-like residence for visiting guests of the university. Lee's image, dishware, and family cookbooks surrounded me. The ever-present white columns coordinated eerily with a student tradition of wearing blazers and ties. My friendly faculty hosts, most of whom were not, interestingly, from the United States, explained that some displays about George Washington were recently added as an attempt to balance the homage to Lee. There was nothing resembling a balance.

When I left the Morris House, I scoured the comments section of the guestbook for some mention of discomfort, some hint of treason to the cause, even just a question about the unmediated praise. I found none. Southerners from all races are schooled in good manners, and perhaps that schooling was operating here, in part. I decided to add a comment of my own. Quickly, before I might be interrupted and found to be lacking in manners, I wrote: "As a southerner, I find the persistent homage to Lee extremely problematic." A weak remonstrance, no doubt, but I wondered how it would be received by the keepers of the guestbook. Did they reach for the white-out? Or did their sense of service to the integrity of the guestbook keep them from making any revisions?

Washington and Lee is a small institution in a small town. Yet the infamous dog-whistle politics of the southern strategy – made use of by both major parties – has been a dominant force in the national political scene, framing debates and policies and affecting elections. In truth, however, the South has long been a scapegoat for the problems of racism in the United States. A century and a half after the Civil War, southerners continue to feel such prejudice that they try to lose their regional accents when moving elsewhere. Yet, the truth of the matter is that white racism permeates the political discourses of the nation, making the southern strategy nationally effective.

Even in places like Lexington, Virginia, racism in pubic discourses has evolved, as Haney-López (2014) puts it, to slightly less overt but devastatingly effective forms. Today, he maps racial dog-whistling as involving three basic steps: (1) "a punch that jabs race into the conversation through thinly veiled references" such as "welfare cheats and illegal aliens," (2) "a parry that slaps away charges of racial pandering, often by emphasizing the lack of any direct reference to a racial group," and (3) "a kick that savages the critic for opportunistically alleging racial victimization" (2014, 4). Haney-López's agonistic language is meant to showcase the "complex jujitsu" that organizes contemporary racist appeals.

More than a few political scientists believe that the United States today might be a different sort of country if racial appeals could lose their efficacy with white voters and no longer ensure a successful continuation of the southern strategy. Haney-López's own plan is to reveal dog-whistle mechanisms as a strategy that has hurt the middle class as a whole. Using basic interest group politics, he shows that the majority of whites' economic stability has been undercut, as well as their political voice. Whites have to come to understand that *their* interests are at stake in the current political climate. But he also makes a more discursive form of argument: that we need to make racism a legitimate, and legitimately central, issue in political discourse again, not the racism against whites – the only kind the right will allow – but the more prevalent and devastating racism ongoing against people of color (2014, 222). The coded ideals of race neutrality and color-blindness, he says, have to be unmasked as the racist traps they are. Though Haney-López has an ultimately more liberal approach to social change than my own, his general orientation fits well with this book's attempt to unravel the appeals of eliminativism and bring whiteness into relief.

Political scientists James M. Glaser and Timothy J. Ryan (2013) offer an ingenious proposal for disarming the political efficacy of coded racial appeals. Their call is to fight without fighting, as Bruce Lee himself might have put it; do an end-run around implicit racism by reframing voter choices; transfer the focus away from anything that might trigger a picture of aggrieved minorities or talk of reparations; present ballot referenda that will not animate groupthink. Their strategy aims to disarm racism without a direct challenge.

In several impressive experiments in very diverse parts of the country, involving opinion surveys on general political topics as well as concrete issues such as school bonds, reparations, and the public presentation of the confederate flag, Glaser and Ryan tested out their hypothesis that by reframing issues to reduce race-based triggers, whites would vote differently. By simply altering the cues of taglines, reversing question order, and changing the way issues are articulated, they show that white vote counts can change up to 20 percent, potentially ensuring majority wins for such critical referenda as money for low-income schools in minority neighborhoods, or affirmative action measures, or just the election of nonwhite candidates to office.

Glaser and Ryan argue for optimism about racial animus but pessimism in regard to racial sentiment (or racial feelings). Based on their experimental results, they argue that racial animus is contingent in nature, thus making it possible that race-based group antagonisms can be deflated (2013, 22). Pessimistically, they cite studies suggesting that racial sentiment, or our national "feeling thermometer," is notably stable (2013, 23). Even the title of their book, *Changing Minds, If Not Hearts*, expresses an optimism on only one side of the ledger, arguably the more rationalist side. By reframing questions in such a way that our racial sentiment will not be animated even if our group identity is, they argue that minds can be changed on specific piecemeal issues. To see how this works, we need to look at the link between groups and race.

The idea of "racial animus" is tied to what is often called "group-centrism": the tendency of groups – whether these are defined by race, nationality, or whatever is salient in a given context – to prefer their own over others, however arbitrarily this may get defined (Allport 1979). An idea that is coming to take prominence in many academic circles today is that group-centrism is hard-wired; not much can be done about this. But what *is* defeasible is the way in which group identities are formulated and the criteria that define them.

Group-centrism linked to the practice of racially defined groups produces a kind of race-centrism, and this creates an intractable obstacle to rational debate, thus enlivening the dog-whistles and debilitating the public sphere. In such an atmosphere, effective appeals will have to work *with* race-centrism to get anything passed, or anyone elected. The election of Barack Obama appeared to overturn this truth. Obama's own appeal to the image of a united country beyond the hue of identity or political allegiance in his famous 2004 Democratic Party convention speech reframed the issues and reduced group-centrism based on race or party loyalties. Continually in his speeches Obama replaced race-centrism with a group-centrism around "America" as a group, but American group-identity is defined by American exceptionalism with a long tie to white supremacy. It remains to be seen whether American exceptionalism will be able to work in a white minority nation where large numbers of the population come from colonized parts of the world.

Obama's 2004 speech together with his wins in 2008 and 2012 has generated discussion about whether it might be possible to reduce race-based group-centrism. In the mainstream media this became translated into the meme of post-racialism, as if we had already reached it, but the idea of post-racialism was not always aligned with the claim that we had reached a *post-racism* society. Rather, I suggest that part of what the *post-racial* idea meant was that we now had an electorate that was no longer as *race-centric* as it used to be, since roughly half of whites were now capable of favoring candidates outside their group.

The emergence of the politically powerful Tea Party so soon after Obama's election appeared to confirm the prior theory: group-centrism configured via racial identification remained an intractable force in any political scenario where racial concepts are allowed to persist. Race-centric group-based appeals quickly eroded support for Obama's domestic agenda, and there were reverberating effects in numerous regional and local political contests.

Given the intransigence of group-centrism and the destructive power of its racialized manifestation, it may well seem as if the only solution is eliminativism. Whiteness in particular, some may think, should not be invoked overtly in political speech of any sort since this will only enliven the tendency to think in terms of groups: whether defensively, aggressively, or competitively. A thinly veiled racist rearticulation of whiteness has become familiar in twenty-first-century discourses: such as the view that the

US is on its way to becoming a "third world nation." A majority minority nation will never be a global vanguard. Many who hold this sort of view seem to believe the fight has already been lost, since the demographic tipping point has been breached. The goal now is simply to retrench into enclaves, holding onto what one has for as long as possible. The struggle for the future of the country and, indeed, the world is then a fight between racial groups. Sometimes the dog-whistle slightly masks its racism by portraying this as a fight not between identities or races, but between characteristics and dispositions: on one side there is corruption, a mindless form of collectivism, and sloth, and on the other the hard-working, self-sacrificing, and innovative capacities. Of course, all these whistle a tune of longstanding racial association.

So this gives us the current context for the counterpoint among progressive antiracist strategists: for Haney-López, we need to make race and racism safe for political discourse once again, while for Glaser and Ryan, highlighting the goal of race neutrality as a shared value across racial differences will have a better pay-off. Is this a contest between moral idealism versus an "art of the possible," as Glaser and Ryan, echoing William Julius Wilson, suggest (2013, 136–7)?

Despite the title of this book, my main burden has not been to predict the future, or to lay out a cogent political strategy of social change; I leave these tasks to my betters in the social sciences. Rather, my task has been to provide an account of what whiteness is that can ground a realistic take on our options for the future. Most pressingly, I have argued that whiteness is an organically produced identity-formation. As an organic identity, the meanings of race identities are subject to change, not fixed forever in a vat of unchanging racial sentiment or animus. This means that a conservative pragmatism that refuses to engage racial sentiment in its pursuit of short-term gains (however critical these may be) will not effect change in the meanings of race or group identities. To change or improve those meanings we have to engage with them, openly, directly, and straightforwardly.

The idea of an all-determining role of whiteness may be deservedly repudiated, since, as Painter notes and electoral surveys confirm, only in its more specified mediations does whiteness offer useful predictions or explanations. But this does not take us as far as the eliminativists or class reductionists want us to go.

I want to end this book with a consideration of how white identities can avoid the sort of group-centrism and group-think that excludes connections to others. This means a transformation of the ways in which some white identities are lived and understood, but not in all – some are already there. I will do this through two narratives about white identity from two rather unlikely sources. Both are true stories, and each suggests, in a different way, the need for whites to have a place in the rainbow, as whites. The idea here would be to transform the ways in which whiteness operates as a group identity. This may also involve a certain deflation through rearticulating new cross-racial identities, but these moves require, in my view, addressing the meaning of whiteness, not avoiding it.

Unglorious Whiteness

How does one find a way to make peace with one's white identity with a clear-eyed understanding of its difficult and painful history? We now have numerous, useful accounts about the lives of people who rejected white vanguardism in both word and deed, such as Anne Braden (see Fosl 2002), John Brown (Reynolds 2005), and Nannie Washburn (1972). Such exemplary white lives need a more public face and should be included in standard curricula at all levels, to fill out the facts about the history of western nations and expand our imaginations about how one might live a moral life when one's identity is accorded unearned and unwanted privileges and a genealogy that includes such a troubled legacy. The lessons of these lives can inform us all.

But in thinking about the future of whiteness, the exemplary heroes cannot be our models. We can learn only so much from those whose lives were organized around antiracist efforts. We need to bear in mind those who live more ordinary lives organized around the more ordinary challenges of life, from making a living to raising a family. In asking about the future of whiteness, it is this unglorious majority who will decide the order of the day.

Recall that the Newton/Goethe debate on the nature of white light presented two possibilities for its place in the color spectrum. Either whiteness stood in for the whole, or it forever stood apart. Neither theory could imagine whiteness taking a place alongside others. Essentialist views of whiteness that link it indelibly to racisms have a similar outcome. But what is needed is to make whiteness ordinary as one among others, neither more nor less, without state-enforced advantage or border control. This requires a retreat from the vanguard mentality, relinquishing the sense of entitlement to the throne of the human race, or a right to share in the spoils of the 1 percent. But beyond the large task of dismantling, rejecting, and removing the accouterments of whiteness, white vanguardism, and white privilege, it requires inhabiting whiteness, and taking one's place in the line. It means even at times negotiating with nonwhite others from a position of disadvantage, as McDermott's ethnography of working-class life shows already occurs.

Bob Zellner is one of the exemplary heroes who modeled a way to be an antiracist white. Zellner is really without peer, but the fascinating story of his life holds out lessons for those of us who are more lily-livered, that is, ordinary. He was, readers may recall from Chapter 2, one of the stalwart field secretaries of SNCC, the Student Nonviolent Coordinating Committee, which was the organization of young people, black and white, Jewish and Gentile, southern and northern, who braved state terror to advance the cause of racial justice in the 1960s. Zellner, as he was called by most all who knew him or knew of him in the southern movement, was the son of a Methodist minister. As was typical of such a calling, Zellner's father was made to travel from parish to parish in rural, backwoods Alabama, taking his growing family with him. Zellner thus grew up a country boy.

The first tale I ever heard of him was after my then boyfriend and future husband returned from one of the Gulfcoast Pulpwood Association union meetings, which was that Zellner had helped organize held in the deep Alabama woods. Since it was to be a multiracial meeting, the weekend event had look-outs posted on the perimeter watching for the Klan. But what impressed my New Jersey boyfriend even more than the need to have such look-outs was Zellner's immediate response when Larry was bit by a black widow spider in their makeshift activist campground. His arm began swelling and turning red, at which point Zellner, without missing a beat, took a sizable glob of the tobacco he was chewing out of his mouth, and slapped it on Larry's arm. It actually fixed him right up.

Bob Zellner's exploits were known far and wide back then, and have recently been collected in a first-person memoir that is a memorable read: *The Wrong Side of Murder Creek*. The story of SNCC's role in the civil rights struggle has by now been told in several books, but this is an inside take from a white guy who started with SNCC just as it was hiring its first staff. Zellner began his fieldwork during the height of the violent backlash to the civil rights movement. Before he had worked for the staff two months he had been beaten and jailed several times and escaped murder only by a slim combination of wit and luck. Over the next few years he endured 25 arrests in five states, and, because the strategy of the movement at that time was to fill the jails and refuse plea-bargains, he was rarely bailed out. While his SNCC compatriots could at least be locked up with African American sympathizers in these segregated jails, Zellner was thrown in with the whites. Inside the jails, Zellner faced life-threatening violence from cell mates on a regular basis, and was also subjected to torture by the authorities, such as being locked up alone for weeks in a tiny "hotbox" chamber until he nearly lost his mind.

The white power structure was of course particularly incensed at Zellner's very visible presence among African Americans at demonstrations, but also just when he was seen in cars or standing around on the street with any black person in a relationship that was not master/servant. Small acts of social equality put his life on the line every day. Every black person who took part in any action in those days, who tried to register to vote, or attended a church meeting, or participated in a boycott, also risked life and limb, employability, and any possessions they may have owned such as a home or small business. They could look for help to neither their white employers, nor their neighbors, and certainly not the local authorities, who were actually organized attack teams set on dismantling the movement by a combination of sabotage and terror. Too many black youth were harassed, beaten, jailed, tortured, sexually assaulted, and/or killed throughout the South during this period, subject to the use of cattle prods, dogs, water hoses, chains, and ropes, as well as guns. The only thing different about Zellner's situation was how easily he could be picked out in the crowd. But the racists, of course, wanted to make sure that he in particular got the message contained in their vicious treatment, a message they hoped would be heard about, or witnessed, by other whites who might be tempted to support this cause.

Zellner's minister father had had a liberal conversion in the 1930s after witnessing anti-Semitism when doing missionary work in Poland. This was while he was traveling with, of all people, the conservative evangelist Bob Jones, who later founded the infamous Bob Jones University. Bob Jones, in fact, was Bob Zellner's namesake. His father's conversion to antiracism was a dramatic move, since his own father and many of his family were Klansmen. The

Zellners were neither well heeled nor terribly well educated, and Bob felt himself fortunate to attend a small
Methodist college in Alabama – Huntingdon College.
So how, and why, did he end up deciding to "enlist," as
one might put it, with SNCC right after his college
graduation?

By that point Zellner had already had a taste of what
would be in store for him later on: the small potatoes
activism in support of civil rights that he and some college
mates at Huntingdon had engaged in resulted in threats
from the administration that they would be expelled. Their
lives had also been threatened for months by the Klan,
punctuated by a cross burning right on the campus. In his
last months of college, Zellner stayed away from his dorm
room, keeping his whereabouts a guessing game for both
college officials who wanted to kick him out and the
Klansmen who wanted to kill him. It was 1961.

In his memoir, Zellner recounts an interesting conversation he had with his older brother Jim before he headed
off to the Atlanta headquarters of SNCC to start his new
position. The whole family well knew the nature of the
storm he was heading into. They were worried, but supportive, and organized a family get-together as a send-off.
His older brother Jim had already participated in early
sit-ins, and had decided to follow their father's path into
the Methodist ministry. At one point when they had a
moment to themselves, Jim took the opportunity to warn
Bob from his own experience what the spectacle of nonviolent resistance – the agreed-upon universal tactic of the
movement at the time – looked like when it met violent
reaction. He also discussed with him the question of whites
in the movement.

> "I hope and I think your personality is suited for this kind
> of thing. Mine isn't," he said. He was, by that time, pretty
> full of anger, and I was less full of anger, because my
> makeup was more optimistic. Jim had always been a little
> darker, more existential. He said, "It's gonna be really

tough, and its gonna be tough for you to be accepted. You know, you can be a part of it, but its really their thing." (Zellner 2008, 123)

Jim was referring to the fact that the movement was centrally a struggle of, by, and for African Americans. Whites couldn't join up thinking they were going to be leaders. Zellner even then understood this, and accepted without issue the fact that the leadership of the movement against Jim Crow "belonged to young black Southerners." He knew the stakes were different for them, but he had his own views about the relationship white southerners had to the movement as a whole.

> But, I told Jim that I was not in this for black people – if this was just acting on a missionary impulse, I wouldn't survive – that I had to look at it from a different angle. I was involved because I was fighting for my own rights as well. At Huntingdon, I had seen what happened to people when they stood up on the racial issue. My cautious professor had tried to restrain us. But he was nonetheless crucified for his association with us. No, I was joining the movement to establish my own right to fight for what I believed in. (2008, 123)

Zellner here gives voice to the view that whites had their own reasons to put their lives on the line for radical social change in the South's race-based plutocracy. He did not raise the economic argument – i.e., that the mass of poor and lower-waged whites were surely worse off with a segregated, fractious labor force that could so easily be played off against one another – though he pursued this line of reasoning later on in his years of rural union efforts post-SNCC, such as with the Gulfcoast Pulpwood Association. Here, though, he does not invoke a class-based argument about what blacks and whites had in common, but the particular policing of white attitudes and practices.

Though Zellner counted solid members of the working class among his family, what propelled him into the movement was a sense of outrage about what the reality of southern racism was doing to black people, but also what it did to white kids who might break ranks. In school he'd been hijacked into a car driven by Klan types his age who threatened his life unless he committed violence against black people. *His own* rights were circumscribed in such a society, and rather than see himself as a missionary savior he interestingly preferred to focus on this motive. Sometime later, while sharing a segregated cell full of rabid white racists, Zellner had some trouble explaining this motive to his cell mates. One of the leaders in the cell – Shug – found it incomprehensible that Zellner would be putting his life on the line for black people without being paid; surely, he was getting millions of dollars, Shug surmised, from Moscow. But Zellner explained that, no, he was in it simply "out of conviction" that segregation was bad for people, both black and white (2008, 184–5).

As Zellner recounts the story of the family gathering organized on his last day before he went to Atlanta, and of the carload of progressive Methodist minister buddies of his dad who drove him to the city, he was viewed by this rather different cohort of whites as representing *them*. He was their contribution to the cause, and their indirect participation in the movement. Even back home, of course, the safety of his family would be tested time and again as people found out that the infamous Bob Zellner with the growing arrest record who became a constant feature in news stories over the next several years was a close relation, and thus a sign of the family's infection. His brothers, he said, "caught a lot of flack for being named Zellner." They made a pact before he left to work for SNCC that they would never deny the relationship and always state their pride in him, no matter the danger this put them in (2008, 125).

Zellner indeed found a place in the movement, and his whiteness was sometimes critically helpful, such as when he could accompany Mrs. Schwerner, the mother of the slain civil rights worker Mickey Schwerner, to an event at the Mississippi Governor's Mansion. In all likelihood, a black escort would not have made it through the checkpoints, and so he and Mrs. Schwerner were able to confront Governor Johnson of Mississippi and Governor Wallace of Alabama in front of news reporters. His relations with black SNCC workers were full of the heartfelt bonds of those experiencing any kind of war together, and have lasted all the decades since. Occasionally, he would find himself privy to a rant of frustration some would make against the "crackers," and he would remind his friends that he, too, was a cracker. Zellner never had a missionary mentality, nor did he imagine himself to be assimilating his identity to the African Americans he worked with: he knew who he was, and he knew why he was there.

Zellner's is not a conversion story. Yet there are many whites who have undergone conversion experiences around white supremacy, and the fact that the films *Avatar* and *Dances with Wolves* became blockbusters indicates that the growing stories of "white conversion" strike a nerve. Given movie audience demographics, these films were not made into blockbusters by the numbers of people of color attending them, but by white audiences filling the seats. Importantly, both tell conversion stories that are entirely fictitious. *A Dry White Season*, set in South Africa, tells a similar story of a white South African coming to oppose apartheid after a series of events starting with the brutal beating of his gardener's son.

One element many conversion narratives have in common is their focus on the high price converted whites must pay in their own communities, including being targeted for murder and beatings by authorities, expulsion by family and friends, and loss of jobs and/or their social standing. This part of the stories is, alas, quite realistic.

Another common and related genre of film presents white antiracist protagonists at the center of a struggle against some form of racism. Whites in these films become the leaders or teachers, and their struggles with violence are visually represented at the foreground of the film against background shots of the oppressed group being beaten or killed. In reality, these are not so much conversion stories as "white savior narratives." They convey the idea, whether intentionally or not, that people of color facing racist violence is old news, since they have no choice in the matter, while it is both more newsworthy and more praiseworthy when whites face violence for their antiracist commitments, since it is based on voluntary choice. Outside the realm of fiction, however, such "choice" is sometimes akin to Sophie's Choice, as Zellner experienced. There was no neutrality.

There are also many true-life conversion stories where whites discover truths about racism. Though such narratives can problematically focus on whites, the "conversion" stories are better, I would argue, than the typical white savior narratives, which focus on white heroes during periods of apartheid or slavery or colonialism. At least the conversion narratives expose the need for whites to unlearn their learning and their previous ways of being in the world.

Surely one of the most dramatic of these is the story of C.P. Ellis, Exalted Cyclops of the Durham North Carolina Ku Klux Klan, who came to change his understanding of race and class and his own position in society during the tumultuous period of civil rights struggles in the 1960s (Davidson 1996; Terkel 1980).

Like Jake Sully in *Avatar*, and unlike Lieutenant Dunbar in *Dances with Wolves*, Ellis was a poor man, far from the middle class. His father was a millworker who died of brown lung at the age of 48, an event that propelled Ellis out of school in the 8th grade to begin a lifetime of scraping out an insubstantial living for his family. Ellis could never get out of poverty or escape the run-down millhouses in which he and his family lived. Through a fluke of good luck, he was able at one point to buy into a gas station, but despite working it seven days a week, the income kept him and his family in such severe poverty that he feared his kids would face the same ridicule he had faced growing up, when he was jeered at for being the son of a "linthead" – an epithet for millworkers who often came out of the mills covered in lint.

While pumping gas, Ellis came into contact with the Klansmen filling up their cars on their way out to cross-burning rallies just out of town. His father had been a Klansmen, but Ellis's decision to join up was motivated more by watching the turbulent effects of the civil rights sit-ins and protests in his hometown of Durham. He measured the collective struggles of black people for change against the persistence of poverty for so many whites such as himself. But for a long time, he never considered the possibility of following their model of collective action.

Durham had been a celebrated town since the turn of the century, a model of "positive race relations" that both Booker T. Washington and W.E.B. Du Bois had visited and lauded. There was a real black bourgeoisie in Durham, mostly from the Mutual Life Insurance Company, owned and operated by – and serving – African Americans, and their prosperity was tolerated by the richer and more powerful white bourgeoisie. In other parts of the South, black farmers who owned their own land and black business owners were murdered or forced out, but not so in Durham, where African Americans could go to college and take up professions. Of course, the majority worked in a poverty equal to or worse than poor whites: both groups worked the mills, picked cotton, and were subject to social stigma, though African Americans were also subject to violence by perpetrators who had the support of the law.

The stability of this juxtaposed misery was upended by civil rights, a movement that swept up the black poor and at least the youth of the black middle class. Ellis saw African Americans making demands and speaking up in a way he had never felt entitled to do. The world he knew was turning upside down, and the Klan offered him an explanation. They blamed Jewish communists for stirring up African Americans with the aim of miscegenation in order to destroy the white (Gentile) race. The ultimate enemy, on their view, was communism, a theory that, by the early 1960s, a decade of McCarthyism and regular radio shows by Jesse Helms, had been drummed into the North Carolina white population. This theory made no sense, of course: it never attempted to explain why Jews, en masse, would have a reason to "destroy the white race." But the theory did not require any alteration of the racist worldview held by Ellis, that peoples of African descent could not possibly be smart enough or strong enough to launch the full-scale social revolution in evidence all around him.

More than the plausibility and coherence of this explanation of social events, however, Ellis was motivated to get involved by the fact that the Klan gave him a social position of respect and a place in society. He was emotionally moved by the pageantry of the swearing-in ceremony when hundreds of sheeted men saluted him, C. P. Ellis, the poor son of a millworker: "After I had taken my oath, there was loud applause goin' throughout the buildin', musta been at least four hundred people. For this one little ol' person. It was a thrilling moment for C. P. Ellis" (Terkel 1980).

Ellis proved to have a knack for organizing, and quickly moved into the top leadership of an organization experiencing a surge during the civil rights movement. Also, he was a thoughtful man, and as Exalted Cyclops he thought often about how to grow and develop the organization. He wanted its activity to be more effective than simply holding endless meetings where men expressed racist wrath amongst themselves. Why can't we be more public, Ellis wondered, attending city council meetings like the civil rights and other community groups were doing? Our worldview makes sense, why can't it be presented in the public forum? Moreover, Ellis was drawn to the idea of speaking up in public, and intoxicated by the private support he was receiving from white city leaders from the political and business communities who would call him in the evenings to congratulate him on his good work and spur him on. He developed contacts with Klan sympathizers in the police and sheriff's office, ensuring that he got the latest information on local events. He had a place in society now, with respect from the well-to-do powerful figures who before snubbed and ridiculed him. Later he surmised: "I can understand why people join extreme right-wing or left-wing groups. They're in the same boat I was. Shut out. Deep down inside, we want to be part of this great society. Nobody listens, so we join these groups" (Terkel 1980).

Ellis had a nascent sense that the Klan was the only organization representing white interests that extended beyond the middle and upper classes to also encompass poor whites. Although he enjoyed the private support he got from white powerbrokers in town, and although the Klan membership was itself made up of men and women from multiple classes, he took his own ability to rise to leadership to signify the fact that the poor had real power in the Klan. Later he was to reconsider whether that power was in fact real.

Ellis ultimately came to the view that poor whites such as himself were being used by the wealthy, and that he had been fighting on the wrong side. He discovered in the course of his public activity on behalf of poor whites in Durham that the demonized portrait of African Americans was all wrong, that they were as poor or poorer than his own community, and that he had more important things in common with them than he had with the white business-men. Like Lieutenant Dunbar, when he made his new views public, he became a target of death threats and community shunning. He lost his place in his community.

This is what is perhaps most interesting in the story of C. P. Ellis: his articulation of the fact that poor whites such as himself had no place to stand, no respect, no real community. The Klan provided all of this, though at a price. He found that his position of influence was contingent on foreclosing his integrity and his conscience.

Ellis's conversion actually followed upon three moments that he recounted to Studs Terkel in an interview in the late 1970s. The first concerned his early consciousness of his family's impoverished condition and low social status. As a child, the focal point of this consciousness was the same as it is today for so many low-income kids: the clothes he wore to school.

> When I went to school, I never seemed to have adequate clothes to wear. I always left school with a sense of inferiority. The other kids had nice clothes, and I just had what Daddy could buy. I still got some inferiority feelin's now that I have to overcome once in awhile.

Ellis's sensitivity to his low social position produced his glowing reaction to the Klan's induction ceremony: the ceremonial pageantry felt like a long-sought remedy, turning the page on his lifetime of inferiority. The infamous white sheeted uniforms themselves provided a solution to his poor man's clothes: under the sheets, such distinctions began to diminish. In the Klan, Ellis was a valued member with a respected identity as a white man. His status in the group was based on what he could contribute, thus making it possible for the "linthead" to achieve the position of Exalted Cyclops. He says, simply, "I felt very big."

The second moment was a small event that occurred in downtown Durham. The Klan wanted to quash the city's likely acquiescence to federally mandated desegregation, and Ellis embarked on the bold public strategy of openly attending city council meetings as the ostensible representative of white interests in this debate. He rallied his troops to pack meetings, hoping by their very presence to intimidate black citizens who had the temerity to participate in open forums about important city matters.

White elites in the city hid their Klan sympathies behind a practice of public neutrality. But they kept up a regular line of communication with Ellis, and he'd even visited their homes, secretly, for strategy sessions. So he was surprised to find himself snubbed on the street by a city councilman he had met with many times. This was not at a public event – they were just passing on the street – but the man wouldn't even acknowledge Ellis's presence and turned abruptly to wade into traffic rather than rub elbows with the Klansman. That night Ellis replayed the moment over and over in his mind: though he understood the need for secrecy, this felt like the childhood snubs he and his father had experienced when they walked downtown in their poor clothes. The look on the city councilman's face as he recognized Ellis that day also reminded him of the looks from his childhood, looks that presaged the "lint-head" slur in their minds even if not on their lips. Ellis realized that in reality he had no place to stand with such people, no status or identity that gave him a position as an equal, as a person.

The third moment was the event that began to turn the tide in his affective relations toward African Americans as well as his understanding of where he stood in their midst. Howard Fuller, an experienced community and political organizer in Durham, was hired by the city to create a mechanism by which residents from both sides of the divide could work together on the imminent school deseg-regation policy, ensuring, if possible, a peaceful transition. Fuller, an African American, had to choose two principal leaders, and he shrewdly offered the positions to Ann Atwater, a militant civil rights activist, and C. P. Ellis. This was a high-stakes gamble: neither Atwater nor Ellis was committed to nonviolence, and both had legions of like-minded supporters. But Fuller had observed them both at city council meetings for a number of months, noting their organizing skills and mass base, and knew that each would bring along a constituency.

Ellis had to think long and hard about accepting Fuller's offer. His racism was visceral: he could not see himself sitting down to eat with African Americans, and now he had to attend lengthy daily meetings with a woman he despised. Atwater's bold and uncompromising leadership in Durham had incensed Ellis. She was from a poor back-ground, unlike any of the middle-class black people often presuming to speak for the movement, and yet she had the wherewithal to make demands, even threats, and follow them through. Durham in this period was no scene of peaceful deliberative democracy: nonviolent civil rights activists were being seriously hurt and some of the youth had started a campaign of firebombing strategically targeted sites as a threat against those who wanted to slow down the process of change. Meanwhile, the Klan was engaged in its own violence and Ellis himself had recently narrowly escaped conviction for shooting and wounding a young black teenager.

What drove Ellis finally to accept Fuller's proposal to share this leadership post with Atwater was not his organizational agenda to make the Klan more public, but his personal agenda to make the newly desegregated schools safe and fair for his own four children. He knew that the middle- and upper-class whites in town would respond to enforced desegregation by simply pulling their kids out of the public schools and enrolling them in private schools, but Ellis and other poorer whites had no such option. If their kids were going to get an education, it was going to be in the public schools.

Ellis's conversion was precipitated by his dawning recognition through the course of committee meetings and open forums that the African American children in town were having as bad a time in the schools as his own kids – in fact, worse. As part of his work on the school desegregation committee, he was driven to the segregated black schools to see the run-down conditions first hand, and he was stunned to find out that their kids were treated as "troublemakers" before they'd even opened their mouths in class, just as his kids were treated. He ruminated on these thoughts at night, until one afternoon he found himself alone with Ann after a set of meetings, and walked over to sit next to her. For the first time, he asked her about her kids, and they began to marvel at the similarity of their worries. They shared accounts of how hard it was to raise children without much money, and how they had to try to counteract the shame their children felt each day at school. It turned out both had grown up on dirt roads. Ellis found himself talking adult to adult, unburdening a load of pain with someone who understood exactly. Suddenly he began to cry. Ann reacted instinctively and reached for his hand, stroking it and telling him it's okay. Then she began to cry.

From that day forward, Ellis changed his mind about the Klan. At first, with the zeal of a convert, he began to plot how to bring his Klan colleagues around to his new understanding, but their response was to threaten his life. Jobless and bereft, he eventually found a position as a maintenance worker at Duke University, and was elected to the position of union shop steward by a constituency that was majority African American. He remained friends with Ann Atwater until the day he died in 2005.

Atwater was the first person to show up for Ellis's funeral, and when she arrived, she sat down in the front row (Davidson 1996, 5–6). It was a service intended for family only, but she had been invited because of her long friendship with Ellis. A few moments after sitting down, Atwater heard a cough and looked up to see a blushing white man who gingerly whispered, "Excuse me, this service is for Mr. Claiborne Ellis." I know that, she said. The man cleared his throat again and explained that the service was for family only. She answered, now with some irritation, that she knew that too. After another moment the man finally asked how she was related to the deceased. "C. P. was my *brother*," Ann answered. That finally caused the man to scurry out of the room.

Readers may detect a note of sympathy here for C. P. Ellis, and in that they would be right. The Latin American philosopher of liberation Enrique Dussel defines the class of victims as all those who are excluded from the very ability to maintain and secure their own lives. It is the community of victims from whom we have the most to learn, he argues. "Victims, when they emerge in history, create new things," Dussel holds, given their impetus toward transformative thought and practice (2013, 355). He approvingly quotes this underused passage from Marx:

> The first duty of a thinking brain that loves truth, in light of the initial explosion of the Silesian workers revolt, was not to situate itself like a *schoolteacher* in the face of such an occurrence, but instead to make an effort to study its specific character. It is clear that to do this demanded a certain amount of scientific acuity and love for humanity, while for the other procedure it was more than enough to employ a well-trodden phraseology. (2013, 361)

Here Dussel displays a critical theme of his liberatory ethics: an overriding commitment to a democratic epistemology. The central role in liberation is played by the excluded and the victims not simply because of their objective positioning within the systematic problems of capital, but because of their proven capacity for insight and creativity. The social movements, counter-discourses, and reconceived institutions that communities of the activist oppressed continuously create are what drives liberation.

Whites who take up the challenge of ending the spread of white supremacist ideas and eroding the white material advantages still accruing from slavery and colonialism are incorrectly understood to be "allies." They are activists in their own right coming into the movement in two ways: first, as "human beings too," as Baldwin's colleague put it, and second, as white people who refuse to perpetuate the practice of white support of or apathy toward the oppression of nonwhite people. The tragedy of the United States today, as well as other white-dominated countries, is that poor people are engaged in daily battles, ideological and military, against other poor people, at home and around the world. The solution will not be found in a flaccid universal humanism, nor in a pursuit of white redemption, nor in a call to a race-transcendent vision of class struggle. Rather, the solution will be found in facing the truths about who we are, how we got here, and then developing an offensive strategy for achieving a future in which we can all find a place.

References

Akerlof, George A. and Rachel E. Kranton. 2010. *Identity Economics: How Our Identities Shape Our Work, Wages, and Well-Being*. Princeton, NJ: Princeton University Press.

Alba, Richard. 2009. *Blurring the Color Line: The New Chance for a More Integrated America*. Cambridge, MA: Harvard University Press.

Alcoff, Linda Martín. 2006. *Visible Identities: Race, Gender, and the Self*. New York: Oxford University Press.

Alcoff, Linda Martín. 2007. "Comparative Race, Comparative Racism." In Jorge Gracia, ed., *Race or Ethnicity: On Black and Latino Identity*. Ithaca, NY: Cornell University Press.

Alcoff, Linda Martín. 2008. "Mapping the Boundaries of Race, Ethnicity, and Nationality," *International Philosophical Quarterly* 48(2): 231–8.

Alcoff, Linda Martín. 2009. "Latinos Beyond the Binary," *Southern Journal of Philosophy* XLVII, supplement: 112–28.

Alcoff, Linda Martín. 2010. "Sotomayor's Reasoning." *Southern Journal of Philosophy*, 48(1): 122–38.

Allen, Danielle S. 2004. *Talking to Strangers: Anxieties of Citizenship since Brown v. Board of Education*. Chicago, IL: University of Chicago Press.

Allen, Theodore W. 2006. *Class Struggle and the Origin of Racial Slavery: The Invention of the White Race*, ed. Jeffrey

B. Perry. Stony Brook, NY: Center for the Study of Working Class Life Edition.

Allport, Gordon. 1979. *The Nature of Prejudice*. Reading, MA: Addison-Wesley.

Althusser, Louis. 1971. *Lenin and Philosophy and Other Essays*, trans. Ben Brewster. New York: Monthly Review Press.

Amsden, David. 2015. "A Peculiar Institution." *The New York Times Magazine*, March 1.

Andreasen, R.O. 1998. "A New Perspective on the Race Debate." *British Journal for the Philosophy of Science* 49(2): 199–225.

Appiah, Kwame Anthony. 1992. *In My Father's House: Africa in the Philosophy of Culture*. New York: Oxford University Press.

Appiah, Kwame Anthony. 2005. *The Ethics of Identity*. Princeton, NJ: Princeton University Press.

Applebaum, Barbara. 2010. *Being White, Being Good: White Complicity, White Moral Responsibility, and Social Justice Pedagogy*. New York: Rowman & Littlefield.

Avatar. 2009. Written and directed by James Cameron.

Baldwin, James. 1985. *The Price of the Ticket: Collected Nonfiction 1948–1985*. New York: St. Martin's Press.

Ball, Edward. 2015. "Slavery's Enduring Resonance." *New York Times*, March 15.

Banks, Russell. 2008. *Dreaming Up America*. New York: Seven Stories Press.

Barrera, Mario. 1979. *Race and Class in the Southwest: A Theory of Racial Inequality*. South Bend, IN: University of Notre Dame Press.

Bartky, Sandra. 2002. *Sympathy and Solidarity and Other Essays*. Lanham, MD: Rowman & Littlefield.

Baum, Bruce. 2006. *The Rise and Fall of the Caucasian Race: A Political History of Racial Identity*. New York: New York University Press.

de Beauvoir, Simone. 2000. *America Day by Day*, trans. Carol Cosman. Berkeley, CA: University of California Press.

Bermanzohn, Paul C. and Sally A. Bermanzohn. 1980. *The True Story of the Greensboro Massacre*. New York: Cesar Cauce Publishers.

Bird, Elizabeth S., ed. 1996. *Dressing in Feathers: The Construction of the Indian in American Popular Culture*. Boulder, CO: Westview Press.

Blum, Lawrence. 2012. *High Schools, Race, and America's Future: What Students can Teach us about Morality, Diversity and Community*. Boston, MA: Harvard Education Press.

Bonilla-Silva, Eduardo. 2006. *Racism without Racists: Color-Blind Racism and the Persistence of racial Inequality in the United States*, 2nd edn. Lanham, MD: Rowman & Littlefield.

de Botton, Alain. 2001. *The Consolations of Philosophy*. New York: Vintage Books.

Bringing Up Baby. 1938. Directed and produced by Howard Hawks, starring Cary Grant and Katherine Hepburn.

Buller, David J. 2005. *Adapting Minds: Evolutionary Psychology and the Persistent Quest for Human Nature*. Cambridge, MA: MIT Press.

Candelaria, Ginetta. 2007. *Black Behind the Ears: Dominican Racial Identity from Museums to Beauty Shops*. Durham, NC: Duke University Press.

Carter, Bob. 2000. *Realism and Racism: Concepts of Race in Sociological Research*. New York: Routledge.

Cash, W.J. 1941. *The Mind of the South*. New York: Random House.

Chait, Jonathan. 2014. "The Color of His Presidency," *New York Magazine*, April 6.

Colbert, Stephen. 2012. *American Again: Re-Becoming the Greatness We Never Weren't*. New York: Grand Central Publishing.

Cuomo, Chris J. and Kim Q. Hall. 1999. *Whiteness: Feminist Philosophical Reflections*. New York: Rowman & Littlefield.

Dances with Wolves. 1990. Written by Michael Blake.

Daniels, Jessie. 1997. *White Lies: Race, Class, Gender and Sexuality in White Supremacist Discourse*. New York: Routledge.

Darity Jr., William A. "Sandy", Arthur H. Goldsmith, and Darrick Hamilton. 1996. "Shades of Discrimination: Skin Tone and Wages," *American Economic Review* (May): 242–5.

Davidson, Osha Gray. 1996. *The Best of Enemies: Race and Redemption in the New South*. Chapel Hill, NC: University of North Carolina Press.

Dean, Jodi. 1996. *Solidarity of Strangers: Feminism After Identity Politics*. Berkeley, CA: University of California Press.

Delgado, Richard and Jean Stefancic, eds. 1997. *Critical White Studies: Looking Behind the Mirror*. Philadelphia, PA: Temple University Press.

DeWolf, Thomas Norman and Sharon Leslie Morgan. 2012. *Gather at the Table: The Healing Journey of a Daughter of Slavery and a Son of the Slave Trade*. Boston, MA: Beacon Press.

Domínguez, Virgina R. 1997. *White by Definition: Social Classification in Creole Louisiana*. New Brunswick, NJ: Rutgers University Press.

Du Bois, W.E.B. 1992/1935. *Black Reconstruction in America 1860–1880*. New York: Atheneum.

Du Bois, W.E.B. 1997/1903. *The Souls of Black Folk*, ed. David W. Blight and Robert Gooding-Williams. Boston, MA: Bedford Books.

Du Bois, W.E.B. 1986. "The Souls of White Folk." In W. E. B. Du Bois, ed., *Writings*. New York: Library of America.

Dussel, Enrique. 1995. *The Invention of America: Eclipse of the "Other" and the Myth of Modernity*, trans. Michael D. Barber. New York: Continuum.

Dussel, Enrique. 2013. *Ethics of Liberation: In the Age of Globalization and Exclusion*, ed. Alejandro Vallega; trans. Eduardo Mendieta, Camilo Pérez Bustillo, Yolanda Angulo, and Nelson Maldonado-Torres. London: Duke University Press.

Eisenstein, Zillah. 2014. "Alert: Capital is Intersectional; Radicalizing Piketty's Inequality," *The Feminist Wire*, May 26.

Elbaum, Max. 2002. *Revolution in the Air: Sixties Radicals Turn to Lenin, Mao, and Che*. New York: Verso.

Fanon, Frantz. 1967. *Black Skin, White Masks*, trans. Charles Lam Markmann. New York: Grove Press.

Faulkner, William. 1968/1932. *Light in August*. New York: Random House.

Feagin, Joe R., Hernán Vera, and Pinar Batur. 2001. *White Racism: The Basics*, 2nd edn. New York: Routledge.

Feagin, Joe R. 2013. *The White Racial Frame: Centuries of Racial Framing and Counter-Framing*. 2nd edn. New York: Routledge.

Feder, Ellen K. 2007. *Family Bonds: Genealogies of Race and Gender*. New York: Oxford University Press.

Fine, Michelle, Lois Weis, Linda C. Powell, and L. Mun Wong, eds. 1997. *Off White: Readings on Race, Power, and Society*. New York: Routledge.

Flanders, Laura, ed. 2010. *At the Tea Party: The Wing Nuts, Whack Jobs and Whitey-Whiteness of the New Republican Right...and Why We Should Take It Seriously*. New York: OR Books.

Fletcher, Bill Jr. and Fernando Gapasin. 2008. *Solidarity Divided: The Crisis in Organized Labor and a New Path Toward Social Justice*. Berkeley, CA: University of California Press.

Flores, Juan and George Yúdice. 1993. *Divided Borders: Essays on Puerto Rican Identity*. Houston, TX: Arte Público Press.

Fosl, Cate. 2002, *Subversive Southerner: Anne Braden and the Struggle for Racial Justice in the Cold War South*. New York: Palgrave Macmillan.

Frankenberg, Ruth, ed. 1997. *Displacing Whiteness: Essays in Social and Cultural Criticism*. Durham, NC: University of North Carolina Press.

Frankenberg, Ruth. 1993. *White Women, Race Matters: The Social Construction of Whiteness*. Minneapolis, MN: University of Minnesota Press.

Frye, Marilyn. 1992. *Willful Virgin: Essays in feminism*. Freedom, CA: Crossing Press.

Fulbrook, Mary. 1999. *German National Identity after the Holocaust*. Cambridge: Polity.

Gadamer, Hans-Georg. 1991/1960. *Truth and Method*, 2nd edn., trans. Joel Weinsheimer and Donald G. Marshall. New York: Crossroad Press.

Gallagher, Charles. 1994. "White Reconstruction in the University," *Socialist Review* 94(1&2): 165–88.

Gans, Herbert J. 1967. *The Levittowners: Ways of Life and Politics in a New Suburban Community*. New York: Pantheon.

Gatens, Moira. 1995. *Imaginary Bodies: Ethics, Power, and Corporeality*. New York: Routledge.

Garcia, J.L.A. 1996. "The Heart of Racism," *Journal of Social Philosophy* vol. 27(1): 5–45.

Gilroy, Paul. 2000. *Against Race: Imagining Political Culture Beyond the Color Line*. Cambridge, MA: Harvard University Press.

Gladwell, Malcolm. 2005. *Blink: The Power of Thinking without Thinking*. New York: Little, Brown and Company.

Glaser, James M. and Timothy J. Ryan. 2013. *Changing Minds, If Not Hearts: Political Remedies for Racial Conflict*. Philadelphia, PA: University of Pennsylvania Press.

Glenny, Misha. 1996. *The Fall of Yugoslavia: The Third Balkan War*. New York: Penguin.

Glenny, Misha. 2012. *The Balkans: Nationalism, War and the Great Powers, 1804–2011*. New York: Penguin.

Goldberg, David Theo. 1997. *Racial Subjects: Writing on Race in America*. New York: Routledge.

Goldberg, David Theo. 2014. *Sites of Race: Conversations with Susan Searls Giroux*. Malden, MA: Polity.

Gordon, Lewis. 1995. *Bad Faith and Antiblack Racism*. Atlantic Highlands, NJ: Humanities Press.

Gould, Stephen Jay. 1996. *The Mismeasure of Man*, rev. edn. New York: W. W. Norton.

Grosfoguel, Ramón, Nelson Maldonado-Torres, and José David Saldívar, eds. 2005. *Latin@s in the World-System: Decolonization Struggles in the 21st Century US Empire*. London: Paradigm Publishers.

Guglielmo, Thomas G. 2003. *White on Arrival: Italians, Race, Color, and Power in Chicago, 1890–1945*. New York: Oxford University Press.

Hacker, Andrew. 2003. *Two Nations: Black and White, Separate, Hostile, Unequal*. New York: Scribner's.

Hacking, Ian. 2000. *The Social Construction of What?* Boston, MA: Harvard University Press.

Haggerty, Dan. 2009. "White Shame: Responsibility and Moral Emotion," *Philosophy Today* 53(3): 304–16.

Hall, Cheryl I. 1995. "Whiteness as Property," in Kimberlé Crenshaw, Neil Gotanda, Gary Peller, and Kendall Thomas, eds., *Critical Race Theory: The Key Writings that Formed the Movement*. New York: The New Press.

Hall, Stuart. 1990. "Cultural Identity and Diaspora," in Jonathan Rutherford, ed., *Identity: Community, Culture, Difference*. London: Lawrence and Wishart.

Haney-López, Ian. 2006. *White By Law: The Legal Construction of Race*, rev. edn. New York: New York University Press.

Haney-López, Ian. 2014. *Dog-Whistle Politics: How Coded Racial Appeals Have Reinvented Racism and Wrecked the Middle Class*. New York: Oxford University Press.

Hannaford, Ivan. 1996. *Race: The History of an Idea in the West*. Baltimore, MD: Johns Hopkins University Press.

Harding, Sandra, ed. 1993. *The "Racial" Economy of Science: Toward a Democratic Future*. Bloomington, IN: Indiana University Press.

Hartigan, John Jr. 1997. "Establishing the Fact of Whiteness," *American Anthropologist*, New Series, 99(3): 495–505.

Hartigan, John Jr. 1999. *Racial Situations: Class Predicaments of Whiteness in Detroit*. Princeton, NJ: Princeton University Press.

Hattam, Victoria. 2007. *In the Shadow of Race: Jews, Latinos, and Immigrant Politics in the United States*. Chicago: University of Chicago Press.

Hill, Jason D. 2000. *Becoming a Cosmopolitan: What It Means To Be a Human Being in the New Millennium*. Lanham, MD: Rowman & Littlefield.

Hirschfeld, Lawrence A. 1996. *Race in the Making: Cognition, Culture, and the Child's Construction of Human Kinds*. Cambridge, MA: MIT Press.

Horne, Gerald. 2014. *The Counter-Revolution of 1776: Slave Resistance and the Origins of the United States*. New York: New York University Press.

Hughes, Langston. 1933. *The Ways of White Folks*. New York: Random House.

Huntington, Samuel P. 2004. *Who Are We? The Challenges to America's National Identity*. New York: Simon and Schuster.

Ignatiev, Noel and John Garvey, eds. 1996. *Race Traitor*. New York: Routledge.

Ingram, David. 2004. *Rights, Democracy, and Fulfillment in the Era of Identity Politics: Principled Compromises in a Compromised World*. New York: Rowman & Littlefield.

Ingram, David. 2005. "Toward a Cleaner White(ness): New Racial Identities," *Philosophical Forum* 36(3): 243.

Inheritance. 2008. Directed by James Moll.

Jacobson, Matthew Frye. 1998. *Whiteness of a Different Color: European Immigrants and the Alchemy of Race*. Cambridge, MA: Harvard University Press.

Kim, David H. 1999. "Contempt and Ordinary Inequality," in Susan Babbitt and Sue Campbell, eds., *Racism and Philosophy*. Ithaca, NY: Cornell University Press.

King, Desmond S. and Rogers Smith. 2011. "On Race, the Silence is Bipartisan," *New York Times*, September 3, p. A21.

Kitcher, Philip. 2007. "Does 'Race' Have a Future?" *Philosophy and Public Affairs* 35(4): 293–317.

Korda, Michael. 2014. *Clouds of Glory: The Life and Legend of Robert E. Lee.* New York: Harper.

Laclau, Ernesto and Chantal Mouffe. 1985. *Hegemony and Socialist Strategy: Towards a Radical Democratic Politics.* New York: Verso.

Ladner, Joyce, ed. 1973. *The Death of White Sociology.* New York: Random House.

LeDoeuff, Michele. 1990. *The Philosophical Imaginary*, trans. Colin Gordon. Palo Alto, CA: Stanford University Press.

Lethem, Jonathan. 2003. "Yoked in Gowanus," in Greg Tate, ed., *Everything But the Burden: What White People are Taking from Black Culture.* New York: Broadway Books.

Lewis, Sinclair. 1922. *Babbitt.* New York: Harcourt Brace Jovanovich.

Linebaugh, Peter and Marcus Rediker. 2000. *Many Headed Hydra: The Hidden History of the Revolutionary Atlantic.* Boston, MA: Beacon Press.

Lipsitz, George. 1998. *The Possessive Investment in Whiteness: How White People Benefit from Identity Politics.* Philadelphia, PA: Temple University Press.

Livingstone, F.B. 1962. "On the Nonexistence of Human Races," in Ashley Montagu, ed., *The Concept of Race.* New York: Free Press.

Locke, Alain. 1997/1925. "The New Negro," in Alain Lock, ed., *The New Negro: Voices of the Harlem Renaissance.* New York: Simon and Schuster.

MacMullan, Terrance. 2009. *Habits of Whiteness.* Bloomington, IN: Indiana University Press.

Maglo, Koffi N. 2010. "Genomics and the Conundrum of Race: Some Epistemic and Ethical Considerations," *Perspectives in Biology and Medicine* 53(3): 357–72.

Maglo, Koffi N. 2011. "The Case Against Biological Realism about Race: From Darwin to the Post-Genomic Era." *Perspectives on Science* 19(4): 361–90.

Malan, Rian. 1990. *My Traitor's Heart.* New York: Random House.

Mamdani, Mahmood. 2001. *When Victims Become Killers: Colonialism, Nativism and Genocide in Rwanda.* Princeton, NJ: Princeton University Press.

Mariátegui, José Carlos. 2011. *José Carlos Mariátegui: An Anthology*, ed. and trans. Harry E. Vanden and Marc Becker. New York: Monthly Review Press.

Markus, Hazel Rose and Paula Moya, eds. 2010. *Doing Race: 21 Essays for the 21st Century*. New York: W. W. Norton.

Martinez, George A. 1997. "Mexican-Americans and Whiteness," in Richard Delgado and Jean Stefancic, eds., *Critical White Studies: Looking Behind the Mirror*. Philadelphia, PA: Temple University Press.

McCarthy, Thomas. 2009. *Race, Empire and the Idea of Human Development*. New York: Cambridge University Press.

McDermott, Monica. 2006. *Working-Class White: The Making and Unmaking of Race Relations*. Berkeley, CA: University of California Press.

Medina, José. 2006. *Speaking From Elsewhere: A New Contextualist Perspective on Meaning, Identity, and Discursive Agency*. Albany, NY: State University of New York Press.

Medina, José. 2008. "Whose Meanings? Resignifying Voices and Their Social Locations," *Journal of Speculative Philosophy* 22(2): 92–105.

Mignolo, Walter. 2005. *The Idea of Latin America*. Malden, MA: Blackwell.

Mills, Charles. 1997. *The Racial Contract*. Ithaca, NY: Cornell University Press.

Mills, Charles. 2007. "White Ignorance," in Shannon Sullivan and Nancy Tuana, eds., *Race and Epistemologies of Ignorance*. Albany, NY: State University of New York Press.

Mohanty, Satya. 1997. *Literary Theory and the Claims of History*. Ithaca, NY: Cornell University Press.

Monahan, Michael. 2010. "The Education of Racial Perception," *Philosophy and Social Criticism* 36(2): 209–29.

Monahan, Michael. 2011. *The Creolizing Subject: Race, Reason and the Politics of Purity*. New York: Fordham University Press.

Moore, Michael. 2011. *Here Comes Trouble: Stories From My Life*. New York: Grand Central Publishing.

Morley, David and Kevin Robins, eds. 2001. *British Cultural Studies: Geography, Nationality, Identity*. Oxford: Oxford University Press.

Morrison, Toni. 1992. *Playing in the Dark: Whiteness and the Literary Imagination*. New York: Vintage.

Murray, Charles. 2012. *Coming Apart: The State of White America 1960–2010*. New York: Random House.

Norris, Bruce. 2011. *Clybourne Park*. New York: Farrar, Strauss, and Giroux.

O'Callaghan, Sean. 2000. *To Hell or Barbados: The Ethnic Cleansing of Ireland*. Dublin: Brandon Books.

Okihiro, Gary Y. 1994. *Margins and Mainstreams: Asians in American History and Culture*. Seattle, WA: University of Washington Press.

Oliver, Melvin L. and Thomas M. Shapiro. 1997. *Black Wealth/White Wealth: A New Perspective on Racial Inequality*. New York: Routledge.

Omi, Michael and Howard Winant. 1994. *Racial Formations in the United States: From the 1960s to the 1980s*, 2nd edn. New York: Routledge.

Owen, David S. 2007a. "Toward a Critical Theory of Whiteness," *Philosophy and Social Criticism* 33(2): 203–22.

Owen, David S. 2007b. "Whiteness in Du Bois's *The Souls of Black Folk*," *Philosophia Africana* 10(2): 107–26.

Painter, Nell. 2010. *The History of White People*. New York: W. W. Norton.

Painter, Nell. 2012. "When Poverty Was White," *New York Times*, March 24.

Parker, Pat. 1999. *Movement in Black*. Ann Arbor, MI: Firebrand Books.

Pierce, Jeremy. 2014. *A Realist Metaphysics of Race: A Context-Sensitive, Short-Term Retentionist, Long-Term Revisionist Approach*. Lanham, MD: Lexington Books.

Piper, Adrian. 1992–3. "Xenophobia and Kantian Rationalism," *Philosophical Forum XXIV* 1–3: 188–232.

Pratt, Minnie Bruce. 1991. *Rebellion: Essays 1980–1991*. Ithaca, NY: Firebrand Books.

Prinz, Jesse. 2012. *Beyond Human Nature: How Culture and Experience Shape Our Lives*. New York: Penguin.

Pulzer, G.J. 1992. *Jews and the German State: The Political History of a Minority, 1848–1933*. Oxford: Blackwell.

Quijano, Anibal. 2008. "Coloniality of Power, Eurocentrism, and the Geopolitics of Knowledge," in Mabel Moraña, Enrique Dussel, and Carlos A. Jáuregui, eds., *Coloniality at Large: Latin America and the Postcolonial Debate*. Durham, NC: Duke University Press.

Reynolds, Davis S. 2005. *John Brown Abolitionist: The Man Who Killed Slavery, Sparked the Civil War, and Seeded Civil Rights*. New York: Vintage.

Richeson, Jennifer A. and Sophie Trawalter. 2008. "The Threat of Appearing Prejudiced and Race-Based Attentional Biases," *Psychological Science* 19: 98–102.

Roediger, David R. 1991. *The Wages of Whiteness: Race and the Making of the American Working Class*, rev. edn. New York: Verso.

Roediger, David R. 1994. *Towards the Abolition of Whiteness: Essays on Race, Politics, and Working Class History*. New York: Verso.

Roediger, David R., ed. 1998. *Black on White: Black Writers on What it Means to be White*. New York: Schocken Books.

Rose, Hilary and Steven Rose, eds. 2000. *Alas, Poor Darwin: Arguments Against Evolutionary Psychology*. London: Jonathan Cape.

Rotolo, Suze. 2008. *A Freewheelin' Time: A Memoir of Greenwich Village in the Sixties*. New York: Broadway Books.

Said, Edward W. 2004. *Humanism and Democratic Criticism*. New York: Columbia University Press.

Schindler's List. 1993. Screenplay by Steven Zaillian, based on the book *Schindler's Ark* by Thomas Keneally.

Senna, Danzy. 1998a. *Caucasia*. New York: Riverhead Books.

Senna, Danzy. 1998b. *From Caucasia with Love*. New York: Bloomsbury.

Senna, Danzy. 2011. *You are Free*. New York: Riverhead Books.

Sepper, Dennis L. 2003. *Goethe contra Newton: Polemics and the Project for a New Science of Color*. Cambridge: Cambridge University Press.

Sherif, Muzafer. 1956. "Experiments in Group Conflict," *Scientific American* 195: 54–8.

Sikka, Sonia. 2004. " 'Learning to be Indian': Historical Narratives and the 'Choice' of a Cultural Identity," *Dialogue* XLIII: 339–54.

Silber, Laura. 1997. *Yugoslavia: Death of a Nation*. New York: Penguin.

Sirota, David. 2013. "Oscar Loves a White Savior," *Salon*. February 21.

Smith, Anna Deavere. 1994. *Twilight: Los Angeles, 1992*. New York: Anchor Books.

Smith, Chip. 2007. *The Cost of Privilege: Taking on White Supremacy and Racism*. Fayetteville, NC: Camino Press.

Sokol, Jason. 2006. *There Goes My Everything: White Southerners in the Age of Civil Rights, 1945–1975*. New York: Vintage Books.

Sonnie, Amy and James Tracy. 2011. *Hillbilly Nationalists, Urban Race Rebels, and Black Power: Community Organizing in Radical Times*. Brooklyn, NY: Melville House.

Sotomayor, Sonia. 2002. "A Latina Judge's Voice." *Berkeley La Raza Law Journal* 13(1). Available at http://www.nytimes.com/2009/05/15/us/politics/15judge.text.html.

Spelman, Elizabeth. 1988. *Inessential Woman: Problems of Exclusion in Feminist Theory*. Boston, MA: Beacon Press.

Spencer, Quayshawn. 2012. "What 'Biological Racial Realism' Should Mean," *Philosophical Studies* 159(2): 181–204.

Ste. Claire, Dana. 2006. *Cracker: The Cracker Culture in Florida History*. Gainesville, FL: University Press of Florida.

Steele, Claude. 2010. *Whistling Vivaldi*. New York: W. W. Norton.

Sullivan, Shannon. 2005. *Revealing Whiteness: The Unconscious Habits of White Privilege*. Bloomington, IN: Indiana University Press.

Sullivan, Shannon. 2014. *Good White People: The Problem with Middle-Class Anti-Racism*. Albany, NY: State University of New York Press.

Tajfel, Henri, M.G. Billig, R.P. Bundy, and Claude Flament. 1971. "Social Categorization and Intergroup Behavior," *European Journal of Social Psychology* 1(2): 149–78.

Takagi, Dana Y. 1992. *The Retreat from Race: Asian American Admissions and Racial Politics*. New Brunswick, NJ: Rutgers University Press.

Telles, Edward E. and Vilma Ortiz. 2008. *Generations of Exclusion: Mexican Americans, Assimilation, and Race*. New York: Russell Sage Foundation.

Terkel, Studs. 1980. *American Dreams: Lost and Found*. New York: The New Press.

Tesler, Michael and David O. Sears. 2010. *Obama's Race: The 2008 Election and the Dream of a Post-Racial America*. Chicago, IL: University of Chicago Press.

Thurston, Baratunde. 2012. *How to Be Black*. New York: Harper.

Torres-Saillant, Silvio. 1998. "The Tribulations of Blackness: Stages in Dominican Racial Identity." *Latin American Perspectives* 25(3): 126–46.

Turner, Jack. 2012. *Awakening to Race: Individualism and Social Consciousness in America*. Chicago, IL: University of Chicago Press.

Vallejo, César. 1989. *Tungsten*, trans. Robert Mezey. Syracuse, NY: Syracuse University Press.

Wagner, Sally Roesch. 1996. *The Untold Story of the Iroquois Influence on Early Feminists*. Sky Carrier Press.

Wagner, Sally Roesch. 2003. *Sisters in Spirit: Iroquois Influence on Early Feminists*. Summertown, TN: Native Voices Book Publishing Company.

Warnke, Georgia. 2007. *After Identity: Rethinking Race, Sex and Gender*. Cambridge: Cambridge University Press.

Washburn, Nannie. 1972. "An Interview with Nannie Washburn," conducted by Sari Tudiver, June 4. Available at: http://passtheword.ky.gov/item/interview-nannie-washburn.

Waters, Mary C. 1990. *Ethnic Options: Choosing Identities in America*. Berkeley, CA: University of California Press.

West, Cornel. 1994. *Race Matters*. New York: Vintage.

Williams, Patricia J. 1997. *Seeing a Color-Blind Future: The Paradox of Race*. New York: Farrar, Strauss, and Giroux.

Winant, Howard. 1997. "Behind Blue Eyes: Whiteness and Contemporary US Racial Politics," in Michelle Fine, Lois Weis, Linda C. Powell, and L. Mun Wong, eds., *Off White: Readings on Race, Power, and Society*. New York: Routledge.

Wise, Tim. 2009. *Between Barack and a Hard Place: Racism and White Denial in the Age of Obama*. San Francisco, CA: City Lights Books.

Wise, Tim. 2012. *Dear White America: Letter to a New Minority*. San Francisco, CA: City Lights Books.

Wolff, Richard. 2009. "Capitalism Hits the Fan." Media Education Foundation DVD.

Wright, C.D. 2007. *One Big Self: An Investigation*. Port Townsend, WA: Copper Canyon Press.

Yancy, George, ed. 2005. *White on White/Black on Black*. New York: Rowman & Littlefield.

Yancy, George. 2008. *Black Bodies, White Gazes: The Continuing Significance of Race*. New York: Rowman & Littlefield.

Zea, Leopoldo. 1992. *The Role of the Americas in History*, ed. and with an introduction by Amy Oliver; trans. Sonja Karsen. Lanham, MD: Rowman & Littlefield.

Zellner, Bob, with Constance Curry. 2008. *The Wrong Side of Murder Creek: A White Southerner in the Freedom Movement*. Louisville, KT: New South Books.

Zweig, Michael, Michael Porter, and Yuxiang Huang. 2011. "American Military Deaths in Afghanistan, and the Communities from Which These Soldiers, Sailors, Airmen, and Marines Came," Available at http://www.stonybrook.edu (Center for Study of Working Class Life\Publications\Research Reports\Afghan Casualty Study).

Index